D1575394

God and Creation

LAYMAN'S LIBRARY OF CHRISTIAN DOCTRINE

God and Creation

PETER JAMES FLAMMING

BROADMAN PRESS
Nashville, Tennessee

4216-35

ISBN: 0-8054-1635-8

Dewey Decimal Classification: 231

Subject Heading: GOD

Library of Congress Catalog Card Number: 85-6647

Printed in the United States of America

Library of Congress Cataloging in Publication Data

Flamming, Peter James, 1934-
God and creation.

(Layman's library of Christian doctrine; v. 5)
Includes index.
1. Creation. 2. God. I. Title. II. Series.
BT695.F54 1985 231.7'65 85-6647
ISBN 0-8054-1635-8

Foreword

The *Layman's Library of Christian Doctrine* in sixteen volumes covers the major doctrines of the Christian faith.

To meet the needs of the lay reader, the *Library* is written in a popular style. Headings are used in each volume to help the reader understand which part of the doctrine is being dealt with. Technical terms, if necessary to the discussion, will be clearly defined.

The need for this series is evident. Christians need to have a theology of their own, not one handed to them by someone else. The *Library* is written to help readers evaluate and form their own beliefs based on the Bible and on clear and persuasive statements of historic Christian positions. The aim of the series is to help laymen hammer out their own personal theology.

The books range in size from 140 pages to 168 pages. Each volume deals with a major part of Christian doctrine. Although some overlap is unavoidable, each volume will stand on its own. A set of the sixteen-volume series will give a person a complete look at the major doctrines of the Christian church.

Each volume is personalized by its author. The author will show the vitality of Christian doctrines and their meaning for everyday life. Strong and fresh illustrations will hold the interest of the reader. At times the personal faith of the authors will be seen in illustrations from their own Christian pilgrimage.

Not all laymen are aware they are theologians. Many may believe they know nothing of theology. However, every person believes something. This series helps the layman to understand what he believes and to be able to be "prepared to make a defense to anyone who calls him to account for the hope that is in him" (1 Pet. 3:15, RSV).

Contents

1

Introduction to the Doctrine of Creation

Welcome to the study of the Christian doctrine of creation. You are embarking on a study that is the fountainhead of all other Christian beliefs. Creation was, of course, the first of God's miracles recorded in the Scripture. But creation is more than the first of God's mighty acts. It is part of the nature of God. God is creative. He is the God who loves color, texture, beauty, variety, and relationships. He loves polar bears and ostriches, sapphires and rainbows, red oaks and rainbow trout, even uncles who snore and children who pout. As Creator He is originator, owner, designer, engineer, inventor, architect, painter, composer, and lots of other related things. He loves what He has created because He is love and He is Creator.

Creation is to God what wetness is to water. It is part of His eternal being, His eternal nature. We understand this as we understand ourselves. Since we are made in His image, we are creative. Creativity, however, is not only something we do but also is something we are. So with God. When the artist and musician are at their creative best, eternity brushes earth with beauty and life. Time stands still. The artist has shared a bit of the inner self. Or again, when a father and mother gaze at their newborn, they are speechless with wonder. They have entered into the Creator's purpose. They have tasted of His power. No words can express their feelings of that moment. The little person who once was not, now is incredible potential wrapped in weakness. The baby is an image of who the parents are. So is the way of God with His creation.

Benefits of the Study of Creation

Have you ever stood behind a skilled computer operator who was "manipulating the numbers"? Changing one number ripples through all of the calculations, changing the columns, the totals, and possibly affecting decisions to be made. What we believe about creation is something like that. When our perception of creation changes, it has a ripple effect on all of life. That is why the college student, who has become persuaded that the universe is a cosmic accident, flounders. He wonders what difference it makes that God exists. On the other side, when the follower of Christ becomes increasingly aware "that in everything God works for good with those who love him" (Rom. 8:28), even the small items of life take on significance. No doctrine of the Christian faith ripples through life more than the doctrine of creation.

A careful thinking through the issues surrounding creation adds consistency to what we believe and cohesivesness to what we are experiencing in life. Sometimes our beliefs have not been tied together. They were arrived at in different times and different stages of our lives. Investing time in the study of creation brings things together into a whole. No single doctrine ties other doctrines together in a unity of consistency more than creation. The reason is clear. In studying creation, we touch upon virtually all of the other doctrines.

Other times, what we believe says one thing, what we are experiencing says another. Life and theology have not been brought together. When this happens, we live compartmentalized, fractured lives. We expend an enormous amount of energy keeping two parts of our lives, belief and experience, in their respective compartments. We are afraid that if they come to communicate with each other changes will come. If such changes need to be made, studying creation is a loving and careful way to make those adjustments. The alternative is to live out our days without any sense of authentic wholeness. Incidentally, one of the benefits God tries to bring to us in salvation is to bestow wholeness, a sense of harmony and unity.

The point is, what we believe about creation will not be locked up only in the mind. It trickles down into life. If one believes that God created all things and then walked off and left it, that belief does not stay in the balcony of the mind. It eventually works its way down to the main floor of behavior, even to the basement of the soul. If God walked off and left creation, He walked off and left us. It is hard to feel loved with such a view of God and such a view of creation. Or if one believes that there is no God, that all things came into being by the remotest of cosmic accidents, it is hard not to feel like an abandoned speck in a vast, uncaring universe. Feelings of futility are hard to keep from gaining control of life and future.

On the other hand, if one believes that God creates and sustains all things through His Word, and that the same God loves even to the experience of the cross, important things happen to the self at deep levels. One has the feeling of being loved by the Creator and of being able to learn how to love. Communication, even a sense of closeness with God, brings a sense of eternal worth, eternal security, a sense of eternal belonging. Creativity ceases to be an isolated act added to life, such as one would think about a hobby, but becomes part of God's Spirit at work within. Understanding more about the purposes of God through studying creation can bring not only belief but also a sense of being believed in by God. God loves His creation and is dedicated to its fulfillment. That includes me and you.

Creation Is a Controversial Subject

Unfortunately, creation has often become the battlefield where two of the great authorities of life meet: the authority of Scripture and the authority of science. Some believe Scripture to be the only authority. Others believe science to be the only authority. Still others believe both are authoritative in their own spheres, but should be kept within their fields of expertise. Usually this option would see science dealing with the *how* of creation and Scripture dealing with the *who* and *why* of creation. Still others believe that the effort must be made to try and bring Scripture and science back together again.

In practice, all seem to accept the benefits of both authorities. Those who accept Scripture as the only authority accept, probably without thinking about it, the results of applied science in medicine, transportation, communication, and other areas. Those who accept science as the only authority accept the values of our society which are deeply embedded in the biblical tradition: the value of the person, one's study, work, responsibility, and gifts. They would affirm love, peace, joy, and responsibility for our world. All of these are key biblical concepts. The believer who rejects many of the conclusions of the geological sciences, nevertheless uses petroleum products in the home and transportation. The unbeliever who puts Scripture in the same category as the knights of the Round Table is seen joining causes preserving life and love.

At the belief level, however, controversy continues to be intense.

Creation is the main intersection where the two authorities confront one another. Opinions are strong. Viewpoints are varied. For that reason no book, including this one, is going to answer every question or speak to every bias. In a book this brief, no subject can be dealt with exhaustively, and some subjects will and must be omitted entirely. What you should be aware of are the methods, meanings, and objectives I have set for myself in the writing of this book.

Meanings of Key Words and Phrases

Almost any word has several meanings. So that you may understand the way in which the key words and phrases are used in this book, study the following carefully.

Notice the way secular *is used.—Secular* is a word which carries several meanings. I use the word to mean the organization of life without God. Secular, when applied to creation, implies the belief that God is not involved in any part of this world, its creation, operation, or maintenance. Secularism either ignores the subject of God, considers it irrelevant, or thinks of it as a holdover from a superstitious age. Secularism is not only a dominant mood in our culture but also has taken upon itself a kind of religious creedalism, as we shall see.

Notice the meaning of paradox.—A glance at the dictionary will reveal that *paradox* comes from two words. *Para* means to be beside or contrary to. *Dox* comes from a word meaning opinion or doctrine. The picture is one of two truths set alongside each other. They seem to contradict. Yet both are true and essential. In paradox both truths are affirmed. Paradox is a helpful, interpretive tool when dealing with truths much larger than our minds can comprehend. Creation is one of these truths. Paradox is necessary because, as Paul said, "We see through a glass darkly" (1 Cor. 13:12, KJV).

Note the usage of cosmos.—Some word is needed to include all that is in God's creation. This word would include the smallest particle and the most removed galaxy. Two words are often used: *cosmos* and *universe.* While distinctions have been made between the two, I have used them to mean the same thing. Both indicate the totality of creation.

Notice that the word hymn *is applied to certain Scriptures.*—Except in the Psalms, we are not accustomed to using the word *hymn* for a scriptural passage. This is unfortunate. The designation *hymn* does not detract from the doctrinal value of a Scripture, but ennobles it.

It gives due recognition to the praise element within it. Four of the five key scriptural passages used in dealing with creation deserve the designation hymn: Genesis 1:1 to 2:3; John 1:1-14; Philippians 2:6-11; and Colossians 1:15-20. These passages do more than teach doctrine or give narration; they soar. They do more than describe; they praise. Praise is a dimension of the heart, born of the Spirit, which is a thing unto itself. No substitute works. These four passages abound with doctrinal truth. They are also laced through with praise. They speak not only to the head but also to the heart. They breathe the breath of eternity as well as build solid foundations for doctrine.

Notice the meaning of new beginnings.—Ordinarily, to put the word *new* before the word *beginning* is unnecessary. *New* means "beginning." *Beginning* means "new." But some distinction needs to be made between those beginnings which have happened before and are likely to happen again and those which have not. The beginning of a new day is an important beginning, but it is of a different sort than the first day. The first day was "brand-new" as we would say. By new beginnings I mean to designate something we would designate as unique: the creation of the universe; the creation of man; the coming of Christ; the individual's new birth. These are unique. To set them apart the phrase *new beginning* is used.

The word man *has a generic meaning.*—For many centuries Christian doctrine has been divided into various topics. These have become part of the way in which we talk about our faith. Man is one of these topics or divisions. By *man* we mean everyone. When *man* is used in this generic sense, it means mankind, all human beings. It includes both male and female. I have stayed with *man* meaning everyone because it seems easier and more familiar than trying to work in alternate phrases. This is particularly obvious in the chapter, "The Creation of Man."

Contrast and Presentation

Take note of the method of presentation. Wherever possible I have used contrast. Learning by contrast is one of the finest ways to gain understanding. We see white best when contrasted with a color; pure white when contrasted with off-white. We see truth best when contrasted with error. We see unique distinction best when we see something that sets them apart.

The Christian doctrine of creation is unique. In its totality, it is unlike any other viewpoint on the face of the earth. Consequently, its truths lend themselves to be set alongside contrasting perspectives. It is hoped that in seeing the contrasts you can better appreciate the truth presented.

Objectives in Writing This Book

To clarify.—Given its primary meaning, theology must deal first with the knowledge of God. To do this theology may plant its roots in one of several soils: history, philosophy, systems, the Bible, and pastoral concerns. Thus we speak of historical theology, systematic theology, pastoral theology, etc. This book uses primarily the approaches of biblical and pastoral theology. As biblical theology we will use five key Scripture passages relating to God and creation. As pastoral theology, issues are discussed which confront the believer who affirms God as Creator: chance, evolution, pain, and suffering.

To bridge.—In the study of creation, a continuing effort should be made to bridge those areas which have been separated. Sometimes the bridge accomplishes nothing more than opening the door of communication between areas long divorced, as for example, science and Scripture. Other times the bridge can result in real connection as, for example, in bridging the chasm which sometimes develops in the mind between God the Creator and God the Redeemer.

A continuing effort should be made to bridge scientific studies with scriptural studies. Bringing Scripture and science together is a difficult and imperfect process. For years I thought it best to leave them in their separate camps. No amount of theology will convince an unbeliever that Scripture can be trusted. It is only when, by God's grace, we experience the Creator's life within us that the Christian viewpoint begins to make sense. However, the trouble with putting the whole weight of Christian truth upon Christian experience is that the questioning mind is never presented the Christian alternative. Worse, the weaknesses of alternative approaches are never pointed out. The high price of Christian withdrawal from controversial intersections is that the best and brightest scientific minds never consider Christianity an alternative. "Unto all the world" means to classrooms and laboratories as well as to continents and islands.

Limitations of space have not allowed much attention to be given this bridge-building effort. I have, however, taken some small steps in that direction. For believers without a scientific bent, this will seem a waste of time. For others who do have a scientific interest, I would hope the Christian option will remain open. I would hope you will see that there is no contradiction in being both a commited Christian and a dedicated scientist.

God the Creator and God the Redeemer must not be separated. Without meaning to do so, our tendency is to put more emphasis upon either the redemptive work of God or the work of God in creation. God the Creator can become separated in our minds from the God of Redemption. The two are, of course, One. In Christ they are fused. The early Christians understood this better than most of us. Their view of Christ was not simply One who came to save them from their sins. Indeed, the One who came as Savior was the same One "without [whom] was not anything made that was made" (John 1:3). The beginning words of the letter to the Hebrew Christians makes this connection clearly:

> In the past God spoke to our forefathers through the prophets at many times and in various ways, but in these last days he has spoken to us by his Son, whom he appointed heir of all things, and through whom he made the universe (Heb. 1:1-2, NIV).

In the New Testament, the same Spirit manifested in Jesus Christ the Lord is the One who moved upon the face of the deep at the time of creation. The Word who spoke the world into being is the Word speaking in Jesus Christ the Lord.

Bringing together Creator and Redeemer in our minds is crucial. If we emphasize only creation, God is once removed from the real problem pockets of our lives. The immediacy and hurt of the human scene are not His concern. He is not like a Father in heaven, but a grandfather in heaven, a phrase the Scripture rightly never uses. I am both father and grandfather. One of the glories of being a grandfather is that, after a while, you leave it all with the parents. God doesn't abandon His role as Father, and He won't. David reflected: "Where can I go from your Spirit?/Where can I flee from your presence?" (Ps. 139:7, NIV). Moses declared: "Lord, you have been our dwelling place throughout all generations (Ps. 90:1, NIV).

On the other hand, if redemption is emphasized more than creation in our minds, faith takes on too long a face and sings too many sour notes. When redemption occurs, creation is restored to its rightful ownership and its rightful place. Celebration is due. When the prodigal returned home, the father called for a party and killed the fatted calf. Redemption was part of God's plan from the beginning, but it was not the beginning of the story, nor is it the final ending of the story. The cross is not the final word; resurrection is. Christ is risen. Christ is risen indeed!

Separating redemption from creation also tends to blur the original goodness of creation. When God finished creating, He called it good. To be sure, creation has been tainted even as we have been. The New Testament speaks of nature awaiting redemption even as we do. But redeemed eyes recognize the goodness of creation. It is not enemy. It is an imperfect friend, as all friends are imperfect. Someday, as is true of all believers, the sheer glory shall be restored without the demonic influences of disease and the like. In the meantime, the world is part of God's creation as we are part of God's creation. There is something in each worth celebrating.

The tenses of creation need to be connected. Creation is not a once-upon-a-time doctrine. Nor is it an isolated single event in some distant eternal past. Creation is something God continues to do so that even salvation is described as a "new creation." The biblical picture of our future, when all remembered earthly things have been folded like a tent and put away, still portrays God as creating. In that eternal dawn, there will be a "new heaven and a new earth." God, whose very nature is creative, is continually creating. The psalmist prayed in the present tense, "Create in me a clean heart, O God" (Ps. 51:10). Every time the Creator touches life, the Creator is creating some possiblity. Creation is not some exhibit in a theological museum. It is a sustaining work of the Creator both for His delight and our good. Jesus Himself said, "My Father is working still, and I am working" (John 5:17).

Creation happens in many tenses. Let me mention four: past, present, imperfect, and future. Creation in the past tense speaks of that moment when God spoke all things into being. Creation in the present tense speaks of God's sustaining of all creation in the present by His will and power. Creation in the imperfect tense needs a bit more explaining. We do not have the imperfect tense in English as it is in Greek, the language in which the New Testament was written. To speak of creation in the imperfect tense implies an ongoing effort to overcome, to be about the task of continually creating new life in the midst of decay. The hymn says: "Change and decay in all around

I see:/O thou who changest not, abide with me." It is well said. It is not just God's unchanging nature that meets us in the trials of life, but His continuing, ongoing effort in our behalf to work in all things for our good.

Creation in the future tense speaks to God's eventual act of creating a new heaven and a new earth. "Then I saw a new heaven and a new earth; for the first heaven and the first earth had passed away" (Rev. 21:1). Creation needs to be visualized in at least four tenses. You may want to add some more. If God's blessings have abounded your way, rejoice for His creation is as good as His presence is eternal. If life has turned sour for you, do not despair; His future is yet to be written both in your life and in the universe at large.

To confront.—Part of the task of theology is to clarify. Another part is to confront error from the viewpoint of Christian truth. Such confrontation should not be to call names or to create even wider chasms. Nor should it be to add yet another label that demeans. Rather, the confronting task is for the purpose of showing the weaknesses of non-Christian approaches and why, from the Christian perspective, they are unworthy of belief and devotion. At the least, comparisons between Christian belief and other alternatives should reveal that the Christian option is not just blind grasping. The Christian alternative is coherent. Just because it is more difficult and more complex does not mean it is less viable. Easy is not a good test for truth.

To exalt.—The hinges around which this book turns are five key passages of the Bible. Two are from Genesis, one from the apostle John, and two from the apostle Paul. Differences in interpretation are inevitable and essential. But may they not detract from the wonder of these Scriptures any more than a mountain climber detracts from the mountain.

The men behind these biblical passages are to be affirmed also. Just as we believe creation could not exist apart from the Creator, neither can Scripture exist apart from the Spirit who inspired and the men who wrote. The inspiration of the Scripture does not rub out the personality of man; it exalts it. Nor does it erase the differences in the perspectives of the writers, but uses them so we may better glimpse the truth He has for us to see.

A final task of theology is to exalt the One in whose name the study is being made. May this study bring to you renewed reverence and praise for the Creator. For the Creator is none other than the Redeemer who became like us so that we could have fellowship with Him. We discover in the cross that He had the hardest part. He will not reverse His original purpose at creation to grant mankind the freedom to choose. To do so would be to destroy the very avenue by which He hopes to win sons and daughters with whom He can share love and life. In Christ, God has spoken in the most profound way possible that He will not destroy man's choice though that choice slay Him. Neither will He give up on His world. For in the arsenal of the Creator are life and love. Even on the cross, such love portrayed its drawing power. In the resurrection, life embarrassed death. Christ was victor.

Let us give Him praise for His patience. He who had the power to create the universe patiently waits as we struggle with the center of our lives. We who are His creation are forever putting ourselves or something else as center and forgetting or ignoring the Creator to whom we owe our being. Is not an audience who applauds an orchestra mindful of the composer who wrote the piece just played? Does not an art gallery pride itself in the artists represented as well as their works? Only in the stance of the Creator and His creation do we seal off the Composer and Artist from the center.

Indeed His patience is from everlasting to everlasting. By His grace, He sustains us. By His love, He draws us. By His power, we are supported all the day long. Through His life, He infects us with the joy of heaven. May this study evoke some moments of praise to the One who is all and all, the Center and Sustainer of all things.

2

The Biblical Vision of Beginnings

Since the study of creation is upon us, where should we begin? By looking at nature? Like the hymn says, "All nature sings, and round me rings, The music of the spheres." Sometimes nature does sing. Other times it growls. Either way nature isn't the place to start. To begin a study of creation from the biblical point of view, we have to begin where the Bible begins, with beginnings.

Three simple words begin the whole Bible: "In the beginning. . . ." The universe had a beginning, a beginning which God created.

"Big deal," you say. "What is so important about that? Everybody knows that things have to have a beginning and an ending." Not so. "In the beginning" is not just a way to begin a story. Nor is it simply a good introductory statement. It is, in fact, as basic to Christian thought as the understanding that God created all things. It may sound elementary; but to believe in creation, one must believe in the possibility of beginnings, especially the kind that turn things around on a hinge they've never turned on before. These are the kind we've chosen to call new beginnings, like creation and the coming of Christ.

That the beginning of the cosmos was caused by God's creative act has been assaulted on all sides, both religious and scientific. A large portion of the world chooses not to think of the universe as having a beginning. In a sense, the first three words of the Bible set the battlefield for the widening chasm that exists between the biblical perspective and competing viewpoints. The first three words of the Bible are the pivotal words of faith. Without the belief that new beginnings are possible, faith is impossible.

Predictability in God's Design

Let us begin our study by setting as a backdrop God's predictable universe. God is the God of predictability just as He is the God of beginnings. This predictability is the fascination of science. When Albert Einstein was asked if he believed in God, he replied, "I believe in Spinoza's God, who reveals himself in the orderly harmony of what exists."[1] Most scientists are impressed with the orderly, the predictable, the verifiably stable. God has provided them with lots of predictability to study.

For instance, consider the incredible engineering that has gone into the making and balancing, the designing and maintaining, of our universe. What incredible skill and power are required to have brought about such existing balances. In other words, as you read this book you are probably sitting down. Your chair is still, or it feels still. At the least you don't have a sense of rapid motion, such as you have when you play tennis or drive in your automobile. But your feeling of stability and security with that stability is one of the taken-for-granted miracles of God's balanced and predictable celestial engineering.

In reality, you are not sitting still at all. Your world is spinning west to east at several hundred miles an hour, depending on how close you are to the equator. The equator moves faster because of the larger bulge. At the same time the earth is moving through its orbit around the sun at over 60,000 miles an hour, and the sun is carrying itself and its planets toward the star Vega at more than 31,000 miles an hour. But don't stop there. Our sun and the star Vega move around our galaxy at the blinding speed of many hundred of thousands of miles per hour. Furthermore, the galaxy itself is rotating at a speed nearly as fast. And that's not all. Our galaxy is in motion also, moving in relation to all other galaxies as they rush through the universe at speeds of one million miles an hour.

This data is memorized by students who study such matters and is basic to the computations which allow us to orbit satellites, space vehicles, and other probes in space. It is a celestial system that is so precise and predictable that our space scientists can calculate the movements of our earth and other planets within fractions of a second. The power and design of the forces which keep the planets in orbit are incredible.

The real wonder, of course, is that you are sitting there reading all of this, moving in six different directions, feeling like you are motionless. For the gravitational force balances the centrifugal forces of the planets in such a way that life not only can exist but also exists with stability, feeling motionless.

Furthermore, built into these movements of our earth is our weather system, so that, ecologically, the planet's water supply is recycled again and again, providing the essential ingredient of water on the earth. Rain may not come when we want it to. Predictably, it will come. When it comes to predictability, nobody can outdesign God.

But predictability has its weaknesses. How many would go to see a football game if every play were always the same and the score never changed? How many would read novels if all novels were alike and all had the same endings? How many would go to hear concerts if every composition sounded the same? Since nature tells us that God seems to love diversity and variety, we may expect predictability not to be the whole truth and nothing but the truth. This is where beginnings come in.

God's Levels of Beginning

Just as it is God's nature to create a universe which is so predictable the science of physics can postulate laws concerning its operation, so also it is His nature to create a universe within which newness occurs. Let us begin by noticing the ways in which we experience these beginnings.

The Temporal Level of Beginning

We use the word *beginning* first as a simple notation about time. We may be up early and watch the sun come up. "The day is beginning," we say. We are simply making a chronological statement about the passing of that which was and the beginning of that which will be.

The Transitional Level of Beginning

The second way we use *beginning* is to suggest a significant transition in life. Some close friends move to a new town. Eventually we might be heard to remark, "They are beginning to put down roots." In this case, we are not only speaking of time but also are reflecting upon a new stage of their lives. Or again, one of our children may have left home to go to the university. We may be heard to remark, "He is beginning to adjust and make new friends." We mean more than simply the beginning of the freshman year. We infer the beginning of a new stage or transition in life.

Beginnings as transitions are easily observable in the Bible. In fact, a good way to outline the Bible is to notice the transitions through which God brought His people. A study of the Scripture makes it clear that God brought along the human family much like parents bring along the maturation process of a child. At the right time, God introduced new beginnings which resulted in new plateaus between God and man. Each of these beginnings is caused by the creative act of God through a chosen person.

Abraham begins the story.—Although we know of faith through the courage of Noah, with Abraham faith reached a higher level of maturity; and a new transition between God and man was realized. Abraham experienced a call to leave his homeland and establish a new nation, a chosen people, through whom God would bless all the other nations of the earth. In obedience to this call, Abraham left his homeland and established roots in a new country. He lived out the covenant God made with him and fulfilled his mission calling. A new plateau had been reached in the way of God with man. A major transition in God's relationship with man was occurring. Usually these major transitions are spoken of as covenants. They are bridges to new realities and possibilites.

Another transition came with Moses.—The transition was made to the law, the boundaries within which the ancients could establish their identities and sustain their callings. By the time of Jesus, the Pharisees had made a religion out of the law. Rather than a guide to survival, the law had become a heavy burden to carry. Jesus and the Pharisees came into conflict over the law because it kept the Pharisees blinded to the newness He sought to bring. The Pharisee's attachment to the law, indeed their worship of it, is bold witness to the truth that good things isolated unto themselves lead to error. But originally, the law was a great and new beginning. It established a new covenant between God and His people. They were to obey His laws, and He was to be their God. It was a vast improvement over what had been. Before then, life was lived without any clear understanding of the boundaries within which fruitful living could be experienced. God's introduction of the law to His people is similar to the training parents must give their children to ensure their survival.

The law, however, was limited as to what it could do. It could draw the boundaries, but it could not empower persons to live within those restrictions. It could set limits but could not redeem those who by choice sinned and transgressed those limits. The law could not love. The law could not inspire. The law could not forgive. When Jesus said He came not to destroy the law but to fulfill it, He was saying that the law was incomplete in and of itself. His coming was to fulfill that which the law could not do.

Christ came to bring the abundant life.—The most discerning of the prophets knew that the law needed a heart, an empowering, a loving touch. The prophet Jeremiah was given the vision of a new covenant, a way of approaching God that would not major on outward religious rituals but would be etched upon human hearts. It would major on forgiveness. It would not be for a select few but for the least to the greatest (Jer. 31:33-34). The new covenant would be characterized by three new possibilities, all prophesied by Jeremiah:

1. It would be personal and spiritual rather than tied to religious ritual and obedience to the law. "I will put my law within them, and I will write it upon their hearts."
2. It would be inclusive. None would be left out. "They shall all know me, from the least of them to the greatest."
3. It would major on forgiveness. "I will forgive their iniquity, and I will remember their sin no more."

It should be obvious to anyone reading through the New Testament that these prophecies were fulfilled in Jesus Christ and, after Pentecost, through the Holy Spirit. God's transition which was foretold through Jeremiah came to pass. This new beginning continues within each new believer. One is forgiven; one belongs; one lives with the presence of the Holy Spirit in one's life.

Another transition is the inauguration of the koinonia, *the church of Jesus Christ.*—*Koinonia* is the word the New Testament uses for the sustaining fellowship we know as the church. The church is to be the support group for those who seek to live out the life provided through Jesus Christ. The church is to be like a colony of heaven. Here the Holy Spirit is able to bring people into the family of God. The Holy Spirit trains them in spiritual skills. He empowers them for service. He inspires them with joy. The Christian way is not to be singular but plural. Within the church, the fellowship of believers, new life is to constantly be reinforced, practiced, and shared. The genius of the

Christian church is not its cathedrals but the dynamic of its caring, praying, witnessing fellowship.

The future is a blessed hope.—The final transition in the biblical panorama of beginnings is completed through the vision that issues from the last pages of the Bible in the Book of Revelation.

> And I saw the holy city, new Jerusalem, coming down out of heaven from God, prepared as a bride adorned for her husband. and I heard a loud voice from the throne saying, "Behold, the dwelling of God is with men. He will dwell with them, and they shall be his people, and God himself will be with them; he will wipe away every tear from their eyes, and death shall be no more, neither shall there be mourning nor crying nor pain any more, for the former things have passed away" (Rev. 21:2-4).

What a grand vision of the end of the age! Its main themes will be of overcoming and victory! Even in the future God's nature of creating that which is new keeps breaking in upon the scenes of faith. God's transitions continue until the final chapters of the Bible.

The Redemptive Level of Beginning

The third way in which we use the word *beginning* is redemptive. Life demands something more than transitions, as important as they may be. A transition from one plateau to another does not speak to the shipwrecks of life, nor of its emptiness, nor of its need for meaning and purpose. The words we use for this newness usually begin with the prefix *re: redemption, reconciliation, regeneration,* and so forth. A contemporary set of words correspond to this same emphasis: *recycling, reusable, remade.* Redemption is beginning again at the deepest personal level. When God spoke through Isaiah to the captives in Babylon, He spoke of this deepest of all possibilities.

> Remember not the former things,
>   nor consider the things of old.
> Behold, I am doing a new thing:
>   now it springs forth, do you not perceive it?
> I, I am He who blots out your transgressions
>   for my own sake,
> and I will not remember your sins (Isa. 43:18-19,25).

The apostle Paul and Nicodemus reached for new beginnings.—In the New Testament, no one felt the intensity of the need for a new start more than the apostle Paul. He had grappled with the demands of the law and found he could not measure up (Rom. 7:18-25). One of the weaknesses of the law was that it could prescribe, but it couldn't redeem. It could say, "Don't fall in the pit." But once a person had fallen into the pit, the law had no word of hope on how to get out. A redemptive kind of beginning was needed, a new creation. "For neither circumcision counts for anything, nor uncircumcision, but a new creation" (Gal. 6:15). Paul spoke to the Ephesian Christians: "Put off your old nature which belongs to your former manner of life . . . and be renewed in the spirit of your minds" (Eph. 4:22-23).

Nicodemus also grappled with this possibility when Jesus told him he needed to be born from above. He was no dummy. He was, in fact, a leader of community and religious organizations. He believed in transitions for, after all, his religion had its origins in God's revelation to Abraham. What Nicodemus did not know was that he needed a radical reorientation in his life, a birth from above. Jesus' well-known comment to him is relevant to all who analyze things carefully, only to overlook a new birth from God: "Truly, truly, I say to you, unless one is born anew, he cannot see the kingdom of God" (John 3:3). This new beginning is of the Spirit, Jesus said. To know everything else and miss this is to miss what the kingdom of God is all about. "For God so loved the world that he gave his only Son, that whoever believes in him should not perish but have eternal life" (John 3:16).

No amount of evidence will convince an individual that God created the universe if that person chooses not to believe it. But when one has experienced God's dawn in one's life, the creation of the universe by a Creator makes sense. It is in rhythm with what that person has experienced. The early church experienced God's renewal personally before they clarified in their minds the role Christ took in creation. They moved from the experience of a personal beginning with Christ back to the first beginning. God's first day became a possibility because God's salvation had dawned within them.

Redemptive beginnings are often ignored.—Our world knows much about the temporal and transitional beginnings. It knows little or nothing about God's possibilities. Recently, the transitions of life have been studied and widely discussed. Gail Sheehey's best-selling book *Passages* speaks of the transitions of adult life. Levinson has written concerning *The Seasons of a Man's Life.* Much of this is helpful. The insights are keen and valuable. But they stop with the transitional plateaus which life inaugurates. The redemptive level of new life is untouched. This is the heart of the Christian gospel. Life can be redeemed, recycled, reclaimed. Rebirth spiritually is possible. The same God who spoke the worlds into being speaks this possibility into being through Jesus Christ.

Resurrection is a redemptive beginning.—Redemptive beginnings speak not only of this life but also of the reality of a beginning after death. The resurrection remains the keystone of the Christian faith because it dares to insist that not even death is beyond God's power to create new life. The greatest of all beginnings, for the Christian, is the hope of the resurrection. Christ, being the first from the dead, promises that He is the resurrection and the life. Death, the great interrupter, has been interrupted by the power of God. Life, it turns out, is stronger than death. Death, for the believer, is a door with both exit and entrance, exit from this life but entrance into life eternal. This eternal beginning, said the apostle Paul, is beyond comprehension. "What no eye has seen, nor ear heard, nor the heart of man conceived, what God has prepared for those who love him, God has revealed to us through the Spirit" (1 Cor. 2:9-10).

The Scripture, then, from start to finish is a book of new creations. They are born out of the nature and power of God. Sometimes these serve as transitions or bridges to new plateaus of faith. Other times they address the need for new life. A new creation is needed. Even death is for the Christian an opportunity to begin again. All of these are made possible by the creative power of the God who touches His creation with His love.

The Paradox of Beginnings

Earlier the predictability of God was noticed in the way He designed His creation. This is a constant theme of Scripture also. God is described as eternal, changeless, "With whom there is no variation or shadow due to change" (Jas. 1:17). How do we bring these two major truths about God together? On the one hand, we are told that God is the God of new beginnings. On the other hand, we are told there is in Him no variation. What we have here is a paradox. Only within the changeless nature of God can change occur. Newness happens within the folds of that which already is in place. Beginning happens within the texture of predictability. Without stability, new starts would be nothing more than fads, fickle whims caught in cultural winds. In God's grand design, both predictability and beginnings are part of His plan.

The God of Predictability

One of the constant themes of Scripture is that God and His Word are predictable, stable, eternal. The person of faith can count on them. God is not moody, capricious, nor fickle. The gods of the ancient myths who argued, bargained, pouted, and betrayed not only each other but also human beings are not the same as the God revealed in Scripture. Instead, the biblical picture is of the God whose constancy extends from generation to generation. The God revealed in the Scripture is the God who can be trusted precisely because of His consistency. This was a foundation for the many great passages of Scripture. The psalmist declared,

> Before the mountains were brought forth,
>   or ever thou hadst formed the earth and the world,
>   from everlasting to everlasting thou art God (Ps. 90:2).

Another psalm testifies,

> I love thee, O Lord, my strength.
> The Lord is my rock, and my fortress,
>   and my deliverer,
> my God, my rock, in whom I take refuge (Ps. 18:1-2).

Isaiah reminded the people of the strength and power of the eternal God.

> Have you not known? Have you not heard?
> The Lord is the everlasting God,
>   the Creator of the ends of the earth.
> He does not faint or grow weary,
>   his understanding is unsearchable (Isa. 40:28).

Christians of all generations have taken heart and hope from the trumpeted notes of Hebrews 13:8: "Jesus Christ is the same yesterday, today, and for ever." There is steel here, Gibraltar-like stability, predictability. We who know our own ups and downs need the God who is not going to change with the weather. We need solid reliability. Instead of the moods we fall victims to, we need the God who will be consistent today, tomorrow, and forever. Predictability is, therefore, an essential part of the nature of God.

The God of New Starts

The biblical twin of predictability is newness, breakthroughs. As we have seen, one can outline the Scripture by simply taking note of the new starts. They ushered in new eras of hope for the human race. We have also noticed that God does not stop by simply arranging the key transitions of life but becomes actively involved in redeeming that which has gone awry. Just as it is impossible to think of the God revealed in the Bible as unpredictable, so also is it impossible to think of God's creativeness ceasing with the first beginning. The miracle of creation was not the last of the miracles. The first creation was not the last creation.

What God did at the eternal moment of creation was to so blend the various facets of His purpose together that they merge in the crucible of Christian experience. Only the predictable can give birth to the new. Only the stable can produce the new reality which creates new growth.

The Creator's Options

Consider the Creator's options and their importance for us. If He had created a universe that was totally predictable, absolute precision would have been the result. Of course, freedom would have been forfeited. Change and variety would have been casualties. Love, faith, and hope would never have come into being. Growth would have been limited. Growth brings change, variety, and surprise. Ask any parent about that! We might add that unpredictability is also a product of growth.

Or God could have opted to create a brand-new world every day, thus ensuring endless variety and spontaneity. But endless change is exhausting. If everything has to be recreated each new day, even memory would be unimportant. Endless change would forfeit stability, certainty, and planning. Growth would again be a casualty. Growth needs the space to change, but stability is the soil in which its roots grow deep.

The way God created the universe is a reflection of who He is. He is neither stodgy, unable to stand newness and hating change, nor is He constantly changing and therefore unpredictable. What God did and continues to do is to create constant variety and newness but always within the sphere of stability.

Consider your own body as a mirror of this paradox. On the one hand, your body contains systems which, when healthy, are utterly predictable. We may choose the menu, but we do not choose what the body does with the food once eaten. The human body is capable of constant variety of movement and the human mind of bringing together various blends of creativity. Yet, neither the creativity nor the movement would be possible if it were not for the predictability of the bodily functions in the first place. In fact, when the bodily functions become ill, creativity and movement are the first casualties.

Mature faith grows in both the soil of God's changeless nature and in His ability to change situations and people. For without confidence in God's constant love and acceptance, we never realize the freedom to grow and develop as the persons He meant us to be.

The Power of Promise

As important as the constant and predictable is to creation, it serves as foundation, not the total purpose of creation. While predictable cycles may be the basic truth about the quantity of creation, it is promise which brings quality to it. *Promise* is another word for a possible beginning born within God's faithfulness. We see this best in our lives. It is not the endless cycles we remember as the corners around which our lives turned. It is the beginnings and the endings. The birth of a baby brings new beginnings of all kinds. It also brings endings, as every young couple knows who can no longer just get up and go whenever they want. The death of a friend or a parent brings endings and eventually new beginnings. Ask any mature person about the key events of life and most will deal with beginnings and endings. A decision made, a book read, a new insight gained, a picture drawn, or a musical composition completed may all be pivotal corners in a life. Beginnings and endings bring life its texture, its depth, and its meaning.

Furthermore, the eternal side of reality gets its power from new beginnings, not in endless cycles. This is especially important when comparing Christianity to Hinduism, as we will in the next chapter. The Hindu vision is that all reality simply goes in cycles. From the Christian perspective, cycles are important but temporary. The eternal or spiritual side of life begins and is propelled by the possibility of newness, even as it is sustained by faith in the constancy of God.

This is why the beginning of the spiritual life is called a new birth. Life in the Spirit is nourished by God's faithfulness and His promises.

The paradox therefore is this: While the stability of the universe is maintained by its preditability, the unique significance of a life is understood by its breakthroughs, though tiny. Consider the tiny, seemingly unimportant, birth of Moses. Yet all tiny beginnings have their origin in the God who created them in the first place. Scripture, when it is seen as a whole, is tied together and progressively unfolds through these often overlooked starts. Yet the paradox is that all of these breakthroughs were born within the humdrum of everyday events. Only through the eyes of faith were they seen and known as new patterns and designs of God. The large picture is a predictable universe; the strategic picture is the tiny new steps that take place within that stable universe. Within the predictable, newness is born.

Which Is the Basic Truth?

Stay with me one more step. Which is the basic truth, beginnings or endings? Surprise again. We would naturally think that the final truth is ending because ending always comes last. When we say beginning, we almost automatically think ending. But in God's great design, beginnings are one notch above endings. If the final word that can be said is ending, then in spite of the importance of life, death ends it all. With this vision, life is a cruel trick. Its promises are simply charades. But the first words of the Bible will not allow endings to intrude upon God's ultimate design. Death will not be the final word. Resurrection is but God's continuing purpose to make beginnings the final fact about us His children. Each ending is but a prelude to the next step. Every exit in God's great design is also an entrance.

The Paradox and the Promise

How does this paradox about beginnings relate to everyday living? In a most important manner, God gives His children the tender balances they need for each new day. He sustains us with His faithfulness which is the same yesterday, today, and forever. Yet the adventure of faith leads us ever to new horizons. Consider practical ways in which the promise of new beginnings affect your life and faith.

The Promise of Answered Prayer

The spiritual life grows and thrives on answered prayer. Prayers are not part of an endless cycle, but personal breakthroughs into the way things are. They intervene. They create. Prayers interrupt. Always they interrupt. They may interrupt doubt or fear or insecurity or monotony. Any prayer, sincerely raised to God, pronounces closure on something and an introduction to something better.

Without the promise of new beginnings, prayer would make no sense. But if God created the possibility of His alternatives within the ordinary predictables of life, then all sincere prayer ushers in newness. Contact has been made with the Spirit who moved upon the face of chaos at the first beginning and out of disorder brought beauty and promise (Gen. 1:2).

Some prayers literally create new possibilities within a moment. Consider the prayer of forgiveness. A man has been struggling for months because of his hatred for another. Finally the weight of his bitterness is more painful than he can bear. In that moment he forgives the other, truly, completely. The burden is lifted. A new beginning has become a reality.

Consider the prayer in behalf of another who has been spiteful, and even hateful. It is impossible to pray for that person and bear him ill at the same time. To pray for another for whom a measure of jealousy has arisen, bears the same result. It is impossible to pray sincerely for another and be jealous of that person at the same time. In that moment, newness has occurred. The jealousy has been interrupted. Prayer, which interrupts and intercedes, has turned loose its power of renewal. Prayer is born of the faith that God's promise of alternatives is still at work. Our temptation is always to limit His alternatives with our directives as to how, when, and through whom our prayers will be answered. But the promise abides nevertheless.

The Promise of God's Surprises

God's decision to continually create means that the adventure of faith will often usher in the unexpected. The Creator is the God of surprises. While part of His nature as Creator is seen in the way He designed and sustains order and stability in the universe, it is the divine surprises which capture our attention.

For instance, aren't you glad Jesus wasn't born in Herod's palace!

After all of these centuries, in spite of the Christmas card embellishments, that borrowed manger outside of the inn gathers our affection. What it tells in symbol and substance about the nature of God! Who can ever say that God is only for the rich, the powerful, the privileged? And who can ever say, God does not understand the "real world" (whatever that means)? Remember that not only is Christ Godlike but also God is Christlike. Christ, through His birth, life, death, and resurrection declares that God's life is for everyone.

The frightening thing is that we, like so many first-century citizens, might miss Him. This is most likely to happen when we take away the possibility of the Divine surprise and cast Him instead within our own options and alternatives. On the one hand we insist we have poor images of ourselves, and on the other hand we shrink God down to our own size. When the Creator does His thing, we miss it because it is so different from what we expected Him to do and how we expected Him to do it.

The Divine surprises are God's way of reminding us that His resources are not ours, His answers are not imprisoned in the boundaries of our imaginations. He has alternatives we've never thought of, and possibilities beyond our wildest dreams. Isaiah's vision is as beautiful today as it was centuries before Bethlehem.

> Who has measured the waters in the hollow of his hand
> and marked off the heavens with a span,
> enclosed the dust of the earth in a measure
> and weighed the mountains in scales
> and the hills in a balance?
> Who has directed the Spirit of the Lord,
> or as his counselor has instructed him?
> Have you not known? Have you not heard?
> The Lord is the everlasting God,
> the Creator of the ends of the earth.
> He does not faint or grow weary,
> his understanding is unsearchable (Isa. 40:12-13,28).

Summary

"In the beginning. . . ." Those words turn out to have far more significance than usually thought. They speak of the nature of God and are folded in a paradox: the changing happens within and not apart from the changeless. God thus provides the believer with the best of both worlds: an eternal God who is the same yesterday, today, and forever; and at the same time a God who creates new alternatives within His own faithfulness to us.

However, not all agree with the biblical picture of beginnings nor the God who initiates them. "In the beginning . . ." is rejected by some religions and some scientific minds. To these objections we now turn.

Note

1. Robert Jastrow, *God and the Astronomers* (New York: W. W. Norton & Company, Inc., 1978), p. 28.

3

Beginnings in Sharp Contrast

Seeing things in contrast is one of the surest ways to learn. One of the best ways to see the practical significance the Bible places on beginnings is by placing other options alongside the biblical vision. Believers often take the biblical revelation of beginnings for granted, neither appreciating its uniqueness nor its relevance for everyday life. To provide this contrast, notice that two large belief systems have no place for the beginning of the universe. The first would include the Eastern religions of Hinduism and Buddhism. The second is a scientific theory which envisions the universe as always having existed, usually called the Steady State theory. Both of these we will discuss in turn.

Hinduism

Hinduism is a many-faceted religion. Almost any belief or religion can find a place under its sky. Nevertheless, one of the distinctives of the Hindu religion is its view of the universe. Huston Smith in his *The Religions of Man* describes Hindu belief like this:

> . . . like a gigantic accordion the world swells out and is drawn back in. This oscillation is a permanent feature of existence; the universe had no beginning and will have no end. The time scheme of Indian cosmology rocks the imagination and may have something to do with the proverbial Oriental indifference to haste. The Himalayas, it is said, are made of solid granite. Once every thousand years a bird flies over them with a scarf in its beak that brushes the range as it passes. When by this process the Himalayas have been worn away, one day of a cosmic cycle will have elapsed.[1]

The cosmic cycle mentioned above, in the Hindu view, finally issues in the dissolving away of the world, an end to a cycle of created being.

During this time, all the souls in the universe depart from their bodies into a state of suspended being. After a period of absolute repose, the world comes again into being, and the souls take up new embodiment in vegetables, animals, men, gods, and demons. After every completed cycle, all things are reformed and everything starts over again. Existence thus repeats itself over and over again.[2]

The Hindu view of creation is cyclical. Everything repeats itself in cycles. The biblical view believes that the observable cycles of life are part of a larger pattern. Creation begins and ends by the purposive will of God. The cycles are part of God's creative will. Their main function, as we saw in the last chapter, is to provide stability and predictability to life. Cycles are, in the biblical point of view, a kind of minor story line. They live in the shadow of the main story, which is God's relationship with mankind.

In a religion where there are no new beginnings, because there are no real endings, a sense of helplessness can arise. "There is no judge and no judgment; no punishment, no repentance or amends, no remission of sins by divine clemency . . . just the inexorable causal nexus of the eternal universe itself."[3]

One of the casualties of this kind of religious philosophy is a sense of justice. There is nothing in Hinduism to compare with the Hebrew prophets who spoke in behalf of the poor and the disenfranchised. Nor is there anything comparable to Jesus' parable of Matthew 25 which can be summarized with these words of our Lord: "Truly, I say to you, as you did it to one of the least of these my brethren, you did it to me" (v. 40). When the widespread conviction settles on a culture that everything is simply an outworking of an already preordained cycle, there is little motivation to change or redeem anything. The ministry of Mother Teresa and her co-workers in India in behalf of the destitute and dying is in sharp contrast to the Hindu culture within which they work. Only those who believe that their effort will make a difference, and that their God has called them to make a difference, are motivated to expend their lives in behalf of others.

The cyclical view of history has a domino effect upon life. When beginnings are removed from the ordinary and normal cycles of life, a sense of fatalism develops. Motivation for change is an eventual casualty. Despair is often the end result. In classic Hindu doctrine, the most one can hope for is to live this life in such a way that in the next reincarnation one will be born on a higher plane than in the present.

This is decided by the law of Karma (*Karma* meaning works), which determines one's lot in future existences.

In Hinduism, acquiesence to life is a basic theme. The motivation to change one's situation or one's society is often a casualty. The late Prime Minister Nehru of India is often quoted as describing Hinduism as an "enslaving religion." Nehru's criticism was doubtless born out of the lack of motivation to change things.

Do not misunderstand. It is not that Hinduism has no truths akin to ours. Some teachings are similar to ours. On the teaching level, all religions share some common truths. But the views of creation, history, and redemption are incompatible. Well-meaning people who speak of religions all being basically alike and all heading in the same direction have never studied the vast differences in some contrasting viewpoints.

Some scientists, by the way, hold to a theory about the universe that sees it going in pulsating cycles, finally collapsing and then beginning all over again. Such scientists find this Hindu vision of the universe quite satisfying. But it is instructive to note that science has developed in the Western world, not the Eastern. The reason for this is quite clear. The Judeo-Christian culture with its strong biblical background sets the foundation for a belief that things can be changed, should be studied, and that man was given dominion over nature by the Creator. Whether science could ever have developed within an Eastern religious climate is highly questionable.

At any rate, "In the beginning . . ." are not simply three words chosen at random with which to begin the Bible. If you believe in beginnings, it matters; if you don't believe in beginnings, it matters.

Buddhism

A contrasting Eastern religion came as a reaction to Hinduism by one born into wealth and prestige named Gautama. He broke away radically from the religion of his day. His was a religion of intense self-effort. It was also devoid of the supernatural. In rebelling against his Hindu upbringing, Gautama taught a new way of looking at life and at oneself. Later in his life, he was asked who he was. He replied, "I am awake." That became his title, for that is what Buddha means.[4]

In rebelling against the Hinduism of his sixth century BC world, Gautama made a clean break. He preached a religion devoid of authority. Ritual would have no place. Reason was suspect and speculation was evil. "Greed for views tends not toward edification."[5] Gautama's religion was completely this-wordly, condemning all forms of the supernatural. Suffering was a critical issue and much of his teaching revolves around suffering, which Buddha saw as the great truth about life. "One thing I teach," said Buddha, "suffering and the end of suffering. . . . It is just Ill and the ceasing of Ill that I proclaim."[6]

Because Buddha ruled out any teachings about anything other than this world, there was no place in his religion for either a beginning or a creator. "What you see is all there is," might be a summary of his complete denial of anything other than this life.

No Savior

For Buddha, the struggles of this life were to be overcome without any supernatural or spiritual intervention. There is no doctrine of a savior or redemption in Buddhism. Instead of beginning with the creator and then moving toward man's place in creation, Buddha invariably began with man, his problems, his nature, and how he was to overcome his plight. Each person was to solve his own problems without divine or human intervention. "Be ye lamps unto yourselves. Be ye a refuge to yourselves. Betake yourselves to no external refuge. . . . Work out your own salvation with diligence."[7]

Some of Buddhism sounds familiar to the Christian ear, for the Christian faith too is concerned with human life, hope, and the overcoming of suffering. But the New Testament view is that all things began with the Creator, the Creator who conquered suffering Himself on the cross and through whom life abundant is possible. This same Creator, through whom life began, is also Savior, Teacher, Guide, Comforter, and Judge. From the biblical point of view we experience life best not only by turning in on ourselves but also by turning outward to others and to God.

On Looking Within

An evaluation is in order concerning the ancient and current preoccupation of finding answers within. The real and genuine problem is not only insight but also the power to use that insight in changing one's attitudes, character, and actions. Insight is only the first step on the road to change. Most counselors, pastors, and physicians will readily think of those who know quite well what they ought to do. The crunch comes when it is time to put that insight into action within life. The Christian answer to this perplexing dilemma is nowhere expressed better than by Paul in his letter to the Roman Christians. "For I do not do the good I want, but the evil I do not want is what I do. Wretched man that I am! Who will deliver me from this body of death? Thanks be to God through Jesus Christ our Lord!" (7:19, 24-25). From the Christian point of view, the power to change comes from Christ. The changes sometimes come slowly. But they do come, and their origin is not within the self, but from the One who created the self in the first place. The reason progress sometimes seems so slow is because the Creator will not abuse the freedom without which the self could not exist. His way is that of love and grace.

Summary

One might sum up the crucial difference between Christ and Buddha in this way. Christ proclaims that we are not alone, that God loves and cares for us, and, most of all, that He wishes to relate to us. In contrast, Buddha insisted that we are alone and that, if any solutions are found, we will have to find them within ourselves.

Ours is a self-oriented age. Thus Buddhism appeals to many who do not want to deal with questions about the origins of the world. The temperment of the times is to turn within the self to find answers to the self. The Christian faith would not deny that there is a need to look within. To stop there, however, is to live with a handicap. For some of life's greatest answers are found in relationship with God the Creator as well as relationship with others. The capsule of the self can be enslaving as well as liberating.

One must further ask whether any religion that insists on isolating the self within the self can find enough energy and motivation within to change the self. If one is asked to look within for answers without the inner power to make a new start, is not this simply psychological game playing? In Christian belief and experience, the power to change comes not only from the self but also from God. Paul's instruction included both: "Work out your own salvation with fear and trembling; for God is at work in you, both to will and to work for his good pleasure" (Phil. 2:12-13). The apostle's paradox highlights the difference between Buddhism and the Christian faith. It is through working out our own salvation that we encounter God's delight and His power. Changes happen through both His power and our effort. The promise of change is not futile. If changes can be made, what does this reflect about the nature of the universe itself? Does it not point as a signpost, or at least provide a hint, toward the Creator who Himself is a great believer in new starts?

Science and Beginnings

For much of this century many scientists have either rejected or ignored the idea that the universe had a beginning caused by the Creator. The hypothesis from which this assumption was made was called the Steady State theory of the universe. In brief, it asserts that the universe with its physical and natural laws contains the whole truth about nature and life. The Steady State theory would see the universe always existing in the state it now is. It would assume that beginnings are irrelevant because what is, always was in approximately the same state in which it now exists. The universe is everything, the all, the whole show.

In recent years there has been a turn from the Static State theory of the universe. An account of these findings can be found in a book called *God and the Astronomers* by Robert Jastrow. The following is a brief summary of his book. Jastrow is an internationally known astronomer and authority on life in the cosmos. He is the founder and director of NASA's Goddard Institute for Space Studies, professor of astronomy and geology at Columbia University, and professor of earth sciences at Dartmouth College. He begins his book with the following:

> When an astronomer writes about God, his colleagues assume he is either over the hill or going bonkers. In my case it should be understood from the start that I am an agnostic in religious matters. However, I am fascinated by some strange developments going on in astronomy—partly because of their religious implications and partly because of the peculiar reactions of my colleagues.[8]

A discussion follows concerning how and why scientists have changed their minds about the possibility of the cosmos having a beginning. This change, little noticed beyond the scientific community itself, may be the most significant scientific development of this century for those of a theological bent. Jastrow has understood this. For if science begins to speak in terms of a beginning, then the ready question is Who or What caused it? The most frequent answer given is that chance caused it. (Einstein would shudder. The predictable and orderly was his arena.) But chance is a poor foundation upon which to build a philosophy of science or life, as we will see in another chapter.

The Big Bang Theory

While the Steady State theory is still held by some scientists, most have abandoned it for what has been popularized as the Big Bang theory. For most scientists, it seems to be the only explanation going to adequately explain their findings.

The Big Bang theory goes something like this. At some point in time, approximately fifteen or twenty billion years ago, an indescribable explosion occurred. The event must have been like a cosmic hydrogen bomb, the dazzling brilliance of which would have been beyond description. The instant in which the cosmic explosion occured marked the birth of the universe. The important point here is not the precise moment or number of billions of years but that it occured at a sharply defined instant some billions of years ago. Theologically speaking this becomes important. Sometime, everything began.

Evidence from Radiation

In 1965 Arno Penzias and Robert Wilson of the Bell laboratories discovered that the earth is bathed in a faint glow of radiation coming from every direction in the heavens. The measurements showed that the earth itself could not be the origin of this radiation, nor could the radiation come from the direction of the moon, the sun, or any other particular object in the sky. The entire universe seemed to be the source. The two scientists were not studying the origins of the universe, of course. What they inadvertently discovered was a scientific fact explained only if the universe began with an immense explosion, the radiation of which never entirely disappeared.

Evidence from the Red Shift

Earlier in this century, Vesto Melvin Slipher discovered that about a dozen galaxies were moving away from the earth at very high speeds. The determination of these speeds is made by what is called "the red shift," a slight change in color in the light emitted from moving galaxies. When a galaxy moves away from the earth, its color becomes redder than normal. The reason for this is the difference in the colors of the spectrum which our eyes perceive. Red or blue for example, are, in fact, waves in space. Shorter waves create the sensation we call blue; longer waves create the sensation of red. As an object moves away from us, the waves are lengthened even further and this creates what we perceive to be a reddening effect. The red shift describes the slight shifts in the redness of the galaxies as they move away from the earth. The degree of the color change is proportional to the speed the galaxy is moving away from the observer.

Slipher, working alone, clocked the velocities of forty-two galaxies. Nearly all were retreating from the earth at high speeds, as if still under the influence of a gigantic explosion. Of Slipher's accomplishments, Jastrow says, "These accomplishments placed Slipher in the ranks of the small group of men who have, by accident or design, uncovered some element of the Great Plan."[9]

Albert Einstein

For most of his life, Einstein held that the universe had no beginning. Later, because of studies done by various scientists, particularly astronomers, he changed his mind and began to think in terms of the universe as having beginnings. Because Einstein is so widely known, a brief resume of this change in his thinking will be of interest.

As the studies in the speed of the galaxies were going on, Einstein published his equations of general relativity in 1917. Willem de Sitter, a Dutch astronomer, found a solution to them almost immediately that predicted an exploding universe, in which the galaxies of the heavens moved rapidly away from one another. While de Sitter's work corroborated the work of Slipher and the "red shift," it is likely neither knew about the other's studies because of the war in Europe at that time.

Einstein had not noticed that his theory predicted an expanding universe. Indeed Einstein was the first to complain about the implications of a universe that had a beginning. Einstein was wise enough to understand that to work from the thesis that the universe had a beginning was vastly different from the assumption that the universe always was and was basically in the state studied by science. In a letter to de Sitter, Einstein wrote, "This circumstance irritates me." In another letter; "To admit such possibilities seems senseless."[10]

Einstein held to the theory of a static, unchanging universe until 1930. The change in his thinking began to take place in an unusual way. Einstein traveled half way around the world, from Berlin to

Pasadena, to visit a scientist named Hubble. Hubble had taken over in the study of the galaxies from Slipher, who had turned to other interests. Hubble had the advantage of realizing the significance of Slipher's findings and of the 100-inch telescope on Mount Wilson, then the world's largest telescope. When Einstein looked through the telescope and studied Hubble's photographic plates, he began to change his mind. He said, "New observations by Hubble and Humason concerning the red shift of light in distant nebulae make it appear likely that the general structure of the Universe is not static."[11]

The Second Law

About this same time the significance of the second law of thermodynamics was widely discussed. The second law of thermodynamics, applied to the cosmos, indicates that the universe is running down like a clock. If it is running down, there must have been a time when it wound up. Arthur Eddington, the most distinguished British astronomer of his day, wrote, "If our views are right, somewhere between the beginning of time and the present day we must place the winding up of the universe."[12] It became obvious that the second law of thermodynamics was leading in the same direction as the first step was leading, namely toward a beginning of the universe.

The Beginning and Ending of Stars

A third support of the beginning of the universe has come more recently. After World War II, interest in the work done by the earlier astronomers was heightened. According to astronomers, the universe is made up almost totally of hydrogen, something like 99 percent. The universe is filled with clouds of this abundant gas. In the random motions of such clouds, atoms sometime merge to form small, condensed pockets of gas. Stars are born when the number of atoms coming together is sufficiently large to create enough gravity to prevent any of the atoms from leaving and flying out into space again. As time passes, the continuing force of gravity pulls enough atoms close together so that the atoms begin to fall toward the center of the cloud. As they move toward the center they pick up speed and their energy increases, which also raises the temperature. When the temperature reaches 20 million degrees, a nuclear fire flares up in the center, releasing vast amounts of energy. This release of nuclear energy halts the further collapse of the ball of gas. The energy passes to the surface and is radiated away in the form of heat and light. A new star has been born; another light appears in the heavens.

This process of the birth of stars can be seen in the Trifid Nebula or the Serpens Nebula, pictures of which are available in most books on astronomy, including the one mentioned by Jastrow.

Other nubulae, two examples being those bearing the name Ring and Crab, both named for the way they look through the telescope, are in the process of dying. A star dies when its reserves of nuclear fuel are exhausted and the star collapses under the force of its own weight. If it is a small star, the entire mass is compressed into earth size with an immense density (ten tons per cubic inch). These become the so-called white dwarfs. Slowly they radiate the last of their heat and fade into darkness.

Large stars are different. Their collapse is a catastrophic event which blows the star apart. This exploding star is called a supernova, blazing with a brilliance many times as bright as our sun. Three supernovas visible to the naked eye have been seen in the last 1000 years. The Crab nebula is one of them.

Thus, the mystery about the birth and death of stars was solved. The ability to study with some sophistication the birth and death of stars adds yet one more piece of evidence that the universe had a beginning.

Conclusions

Three differing scientific approaches have led to the same conclusion. The universe had a beginning. The first evidence is that the universe is expanding as evidenced by the red shift. The second is of the second law of thermodynamics, which declares that the universe will someday come to an end. The third is the observation of the birth and death of stars.

Please notice that science and Scripture do not always lead in opposite directions. Truth is truth wherever it is found. Since we believe in a Creator, all roads are eventually going to lead back to the same conclusions.

Notice also that even scientists can become very dogmatic when their viewpoints are threatened. Not all scientists have been enthusiastic about this correlation between their findings and the doctrine of beginnings. Eddington wrote in 1931, "I have no axe to grind in this discussion," but "the notion of a beginning is repugnant to me."[13]

Walter Nernst, a German chemist, was vehement in his denial of this most recent scientific finding: "To deny the infinite duration of time would be to betray the very foundation of science."[14] Allan Sandage of Palomar Observatory, who himself established the uniformity of the expansion of the universe, said, "It is such a strange conclusion . . . it cannot really be true."[15] What we have here is a reverse of the Galileo incident when the church fathers would not look into Galileo's telescope lest they see something they could not believe. Apparantly scientists are not always free of dogmatism either. Jastrow remarks:

> Theologians generally are delighted with the proof that the Universe had a beginning, but astronomers are curiously upset. Their reactions provide an interesting demonstration of the response of the scientific mind—supposedly a very objective mind—when evidence uncovered by science itself leads to a conflict with the articles of faith of our profession. It turns out that the scientist behaves the way the rest of us do when our beliefs are in conflict with the evidence. We become irritated, we pretend the conflict does not exist, or we paper it over with meaningless phrases.[16]

In the same way, some Christian believers are inclined to scoff at scientific postulations concerning births and deaths of stars and all other scientific findings which they cannot understand. Like the dogmatic scientists, they do not wish to enlarge their vision to include both biblical truth and scientific investigation. Remember, God gave us the responsibility to have dominion over creation (Gen. 1:28). Part of the joy of scientific discovery is the thrill of finding out more about God's creations. As both believers and scientists find, there are some surprises from the God who delights in surprises. As believers, we do well to remember that science is no threat to faith unless our view of God is too small or our fear of science is too large.

Notice finally what science is doing with this new understanding. We could wish that this discovery would bring a willingness to take another look at the evidence for the Creator. Unfortunately this has not often happened. Instead, science often welds itself to a secular creed which intends to organize life and thought without reference to God.

For the believer, it is important to appreciate anew a faith that breathes the air of possibility and new beginnings. Let us rejoice in science for it, too, is part of God's world. Let us give thanks for the many benefits it has brought us. Perhaps someday those who reject the Christian viewpoint will give consideration to the benefits faith could bring them. In the meantime, let us remember that faith is not dependent upon discoveries by science past, present, or future. It is sustained by the One who is the same yesterday, today, and forever.

Notes

1. Huston Smith, *The Religions of Man* (New York: Mentor Books, 1958), p. 81.
2. John B. Noss, *Man's Religions* (New York: The Macmillan Company, 1961), p. 134.
3. Ibid., p. 135.
4. Smith, p. 90.
5. Ibid., p. 103
6. Ibid., p. 106.
7. Ibid., p. 107.
8. Robert Jastrow, *God and the Astronomers* (New York: W. W. Norton & Company, Inc., 1978), p. 11.
9. Ibid., p. 29.
10. Ibid., p. 27-8.
11. Ibid., p. 48.
12. Ibid.
13. Ibid., p. 112.
14. Ibid.
15. Ibid.
16. Ibid., p. 16.

4

The Creation of the Universe

The silence of eternity was ended. Immense energy and power were unleashed such as eternity had never known before. Out into the immense unthinkable spaces, filling unknowable voids, in spectacular color and designs, the universe began to take shape. In typical understatement the Bible says simply, "In the beginning God created the heavens and the earth" (Gen. 1:1).

In the beginning our God, who is described as love, created. What it means to create as God creates we can only meagerly imagine. But in that pristine moment, God became Inventor, Designer, Programmer, Ecologist, and Engineer on a scale and in ways that boggle the mind. When we begin to perceive the immensity of it, the sheer grandeur, the intricate planning, awe and mystery capture us. We stand breathless at the glory and wonder of creation. Our verbal analogies fail. Our descriptive metaphors turn out to be inadequate.

The Universe Is Divine Size

When we first begin to study the heavens, the galaxies, the immense distances measured in light years, we are overwhelmed. This is understandable. Not too long ago, the human race took for granted that the stars we can see at night were the only stars in the heavens. We thought the sun revolved around the earth and that our beautiful earth was the center of everything. For us to get used to a universe that is so large that it stretches every known metaphor takes some time.

But instead of being overcome by the vastness of the universe, look at it this way. If God is as great as we claim He is, wouldn't we be disappointed if He came up with a meager Roman-candle-like universe? When God created His universe, He did it divine size. That is, He planned its immensity, and He planned its minutiae. The immensity of the universe is no more miraculous than the atom, but this greatness can threaten us when we are accosted by its vastness.

Take another look. God's immense spaces are for a purpose. To have precise order in the laws of creation takes space. It is rather like a secretary whose office is suddenly innundated by files upon files. It is not orderly. It is mass confusion. What is needed is more space so that everything can have its space and its order. Or again, it is something like a family living in a house that is much smaller than required. Order and organization are not words that characterize them when they are all together. They need more space, and with more space a sense of order returns. The universe is so vast because God is the God of intricate design and incredible order. He created space for things to happen and for orbits to occur, for stars to be born and for planets to find their niche. The universe is not too big. Our view of God is too small.

Part of our problem with the size of the universe has to do with our egos. To find that ours is not the only galaxy, and that our earth is not even the center of our galaxy, is a little deflating. Such, however, is the consistent pattern of God. It was not in Rome or Athens that the Savior was born but in tiny, back-side-of-nowhere Bethlehem. Our Lord would memorialize the Sea of Galilee but it is not a sea as seas go. By most dimensions, it is a good-sized lake. During His ministry, He never traveled farther than some commute to work today. He never had a press conference and never wrote a book. That our earth should be where it is in our galaxy and that our galaxy should be where it is among the other galaxies would seem consistent to God's pattern. God seems to enjoy placing things in nooks and crannies. The size of God's universe is our problem, not His.

Still, we have a good place to begin inasmuch as the Bible begins with a magnificent account of creation. It is full of praise and worthy of the title "hymn." If you don't like the designation "hymn," call it a praise account. For Genesis 1 is an incredible piece of revelation to us about the nature of creation and the God who creates. The offering of praise begins: "In the beginning God created the heavens and the earth" (Gen. 1:1).

A Theologian and Scientist

When we read Genesis 1, we are brushing against two awe-inspiring phenomena. The first is the work of the Holy Spirit in inspiring the words so that each generation would find them relevant, corrective, and visionary. The second is the remarkable man through whom the Holy Spirit wrote. What a mind he had. He had the gift to perceive what we would call scientific order. He grasped the issues of faith that were upon him. His was so spiritually sensitive and creative that he stepped out of the culture and background of his era. How difficult that is to do. His basic perceptions of the order and progression of creation were ahead of its time.

Consider the amazing phenomenon that, when our three astronauts were on their way to the moon in 1969, they chose during that Christmas season the reading of Genesis 1. That remarkable person who first received the revelation we call Genesis 1 could scarcely have believed the kind of world we live in: television, satellites, air travel, instant communication. Yet his words remain like a guiding North Star in the midst of a darkened and troubled sky.

To have the respect of every age, the words of Genesis 1 had to be simple enough for the common person to understand. Yet they had to be vivid enough to command the attention of the ages. Scientific jargon, as well as theological complexity, would have to be omitted. Suppose, for example, scientific words were placed in the account. They would have been unintelligible for centuries. Besides, the vocabulary of science is in constant change. If it had used the language of one era, it would have missed the others. If Genesis 1 had communicated only the theology of its own era, it would have been dismissed by both Hebrew and Christian thinkers of later centuries. Instead, what the chapter does is portray in vivid images the basic vision of creation which has become part of the heritage of faith through the years.

Leaning Against Primitive Winds

Genesis was not written in a vacuum. Then, as now, prevailing viewpoints about the world and its beginnings captured the minds of the populace. Such viewpoints are sometimes called *world views.* What prevailing world view existed in the early primitive world?

Ancient historical research has now compiled over five thousand tablets or fragments of the literary skills of the Sumerian civilization which existed during the third and fourth centuries before Christ. Civilization as we know it is often described as having begun during this time.[1] The prevailing viewpoints of that era were in direct contrast to the view we find in Genesis. It is obvious that Genesis 1 and 2 were written to argue for another position. Some of these direct contrasts are summarized as follows.

God Is One God

All of the ancient myths of creation are polytheistic. That is, they believed in many gods. These gods argued and plotted against each other. Inherent in polytheism is the tendency for people to try to satisfy all gods, offending none, lest the displeasure of one neglected god bring reprisal. All sorts of religious rituals were, therefore, created to placate or satisfy the gods and their many, sometimes contradictory, demands.

In contrast, the biblical Creator is One. He is the origin and the cause of all things. The parts of creation that primitive religion tended to worship are all said to be created by God and His Word. Notice particularly in the biblical account that light was created before the creation of the sun and the moon or any of the stars or constellation of stars. Not only is this the way science proposes that it happened but also it is in direct contrast with the polytheism of the ancient world which worshiped sun, moon, or the constellations. The writer, in fact, wouldn't even name them, wouldn't even give them the honor of their identification. Only "God made the two great lights, the greater light to rule the day, and the lesser light to rule the night" (Gen. 1:16). The refusal to identify any of the constellations is a direct argument against ancient astrology which, then as now, was assumed to control everything from the heavens.

God Creates and Sustains All Things Through His Word

Research about ancient religions shows that the religious festivals were not only for the gathering of the faithful but were actually thought to sustain the universe as the people understood it. The people's faithful attendance at and observance of the festivals were believed essential to the preservation of life. The reciting of their religious beliefs were thought to keep the world going.[2]

In contrast, the Bible insists that all things were created by God's word and continue to be sustained by that word. I feel that Genesis 1 is best understood as one long hymn of praise to the God to whom all things owe their being. Magic plays no part. Nor is there anything people can do to keep the universe going. All of creation is created and sustained by the God whose word spoke the universe into being.

In the New Testament, the same declaration was made of our Lord. Of Him it is written: "In the beginning was the Word, and the Word was with God, and the Word was God. He was in the beginning with God; all things were made through him, and without him was not anything made that was made" (John 1:1-2).

God even created the great sea monsters (Gen. 1:21). The modern reader is apt to read that and shrug it off as being an early belief in sea monsters. Thus we miss the point. An important affirmation is being made here. Ancient mythologies often believed the sea monsters to possess independent powers of their own and often feared them as sources of destruction and chaos. Instead, the Bible puts them in their place. Not only does God create them, but He plays with them (Ps. 104:26, NEB) and deserves their praise (Ps. 148:7).

Other differences abound, but this illustrates that the Genesis praise accounts were contradicting the mythical beliefs of their day. Some writers have pointed out that the Genesis 1 account was dependent upon earlier mythical and polytheistic versions because some of the words are similar. Nonsense. There are always only so many words in any language that a person can use, especically if one desires to be understood. Believers and unbelievers alike often use the same words. Because a modern minister uses the word *self* does not mean he believes in worshiping the self. Any honest look at the comparision between Genesis and the ancient myths will reveal that Genesis was leaning against the prevailing winds of time.

Theological Foundations of Genesis 1

If the writer of the Genesis 1 praise account of creation were in one of our universities today, he would likely excel in science and math. That he would ever find his way to the religion department is remote, campuses being as compartmentalized as they are. Fortunately, the age in which he lived had not separated the study of the universe from the study of God. Consequently his vision of God's beginning of the cosmos is not only an orderly account of how creation happened but also builds the foundations upon which all later theology would be built. To these foundations we now turn.

The Source of All Creation Is God

There is no effort to prove God nor to give evidences of His existence. "God created" serves as introduction and gospel. No proof of God can be given if He is the Author of all that is. We can no more "prove" His existence than a person pictured in a photograph can step out and prove the existence of the photographer. The existence of the photographer is assumed. We can no more "prove" His existence than the character of a novel can step outside the novel and prove the existence of the author. The existence of the novelist is assumed. To the writer of these ancient words, and to all believers since, the fact that God created becomes the fountainhead and the conclusion of all that issues from personal experience with the living God.

The Hebrew word used for God's act of creation is carefully chosen and deliberate. It is *bara. Bara* is used sparingly in the Old Testament. It is used of those instances when something new came into being. It was a favorite word of the prophet Isaiah. Of the many times he used it, it always refers to something new that God is going to do. In Genesis 1, it teams with God's word to set the rest of creation apart from man. For how shall it be said that God has created? He did not fashion the clay as a potter works with a wheel, nor compose like a musician at the piano, nor work like a sculptor on preexisting material. All analogies fail. For how is God said to "create"? How does one begin to comprehend God creating the universe out of nothing? The declaration is made that He spoke it into being through His Word.

The science and culture of our era have great problems affirming that a personal deity is at the headwaters of all things. "God created" is not one of the phrases they use. The origin of our world is thought of as arising from random chance and impersonal forces. A chapter is devoted to these concepts later in this book. Nevertheless, it is impossible to ignore the question of origin. When science does talk in terms of that moment when all things began, they inevitably have to talk in terms of who or what or whatever.

Clifford C. Simak, in his book *Wonder and Glory,* tells the story of the universe from the scientific point of view. In the later chapters, he discusses the origin of the universe. Insofar as I was able to tell, he never uses the word *God.* He restricts his discussion completely to the material aspects of creation. "We might imagine, in addition to the material universe, an immaterial universe, that would include all intellectual and theological concepts and all emotions. About this immaterial universe there is nothing we can say here, for it lies outside the realm of the kind of science we are here concerned with."[3] Yet later in the same chapter, Simak faces that tough, Gibraltar-like question about the origin of matter.

> Whence came this great blob of matter that made up the cosmic egg? It had to come into being somewhere, at some time, under certain precise conditions. There had to be operative physical laws under which it was possible for it to be created. It is not necessary to believe that the universe was created in any particular manner, but it is necessary to believe that somewhere, somehow, matter was created. It is one of those basic things that at the moment seems unanswerable.[4]

First cause is what some ancients used to call it. What was the first something or Someone that caused everything? For the man of faith who wrote Genesis 1, his simple declaration was, "In the beginning God created. . . ." Without that one affirmation to build on, all theology is impossible.

The Spiritual Order Precedes and Transcends the Material

By the second verse in the Bible, we have been introduced to the idea of the spiritual order and the power of the Spirit of God. "The earth was without form and void, and darkness was upon the face of the deep; and the Spirit of God was moving over the face of the waters." That there is a reality over and above and apart from matter, a reality the Scripture calls Spirit, is a basic affirmation of the Christian faith. In a materialistic culture, the spiritual is often abandoned, ignored, or suspected. For many, the battle for belief is won only when there develops a conviction that what we see or can study is not all that there is. This indispensible foundation of faith is expressed forcefully by Paul to the Corinthians: "We look not to the things that are seen but to the things that are unseen; for the things that are seen are transient, but the things that are unseen are eternal" (2 Cor. 4:18).

Morton Kelsey has done us all a favor by outlining the steps whereby the spiritual reality has become suspect even in some theological thinking. Of more interest to the layman, he has gone through the New Testament and carefully totaled the number of verses that are related to distinctly spiritual experiences. Out of the 7,957 verses in the New Testament, 3,874 fit into the spiritual experience category.[5] Biblical faith vibrates with the Spirit of God at work in His world. The theologian-scientist who composed Genesis 1 built the foundation upon which all later biblical teachings about the Spirit of God are built.

The earliest picture of the Spirit's moving is to act upon and do something with that which was "without form and void." The words are *formless* (*tohu*) and *empty* (*bohu*). The words *formless* and *empty* are not only words to describe what was before creation but also to describe what was and is without the presence of the Spirit. A society which has rejected its spiritual roots begins to take on characteristics that can be described as formless and empty. T. S. Eliot as far back as 1925 was using phrases of our world like "Shape without form, shade without colour, Paralysed force, gesture without motion."[6] These words of emptiness describe our society, engineered for everything but the Spirit who fills and forms paths of meaning and fulfillment.

Three words which describe the work of the Spirit are *form, fill,* and *finish.* The work of the Spirit continues to form and to fill with the purpose of finishing that which formerly could have been but was not. Our world could use a little forming, filling, and finishing. The pattern of the Spirit is consistent whether it be in creating the universe, society, church, or an individual life.

One word of caution. Just because the spiritual realm (Gen. 1:2) precedes and is transcendent to the material order does not mean God left them apart. In fact one of the great truths of both Old and New Testaments is that God works within and through the created order to achieve His own purposes for His world and His people. To that principle we now turn.

God Works Within the Created Order, Not Apart from It

Some religions, especially Buddhism, have little patience with the created order of things. For believers in such religions, salvation comes not from within the created order but in somehow rising above it. Sometimes Christians can get into that same thought pattern. They think what exists in the world is evil. Their premise is that only by withdrawing from the world can any kind of spiritual life be found.

The grand vision of the theologian-scientist is that God's purposes will be realized through the created order and not apart from it. God's great creative effort is to fuse, so to speak, the spiritual and the material and make them one. Only of man is the designation given, "made in the image of God." But that does not mean he descends from another created order, from another planet, or is apart from the rest of creation. Instead, man is created, in God's pattern of things, out of the dust of the earth. Image and earth are not separated. God's commitment to the created order reached its full fruition in Jesus Christ our Lord, who came through a mother's womb, as a baby, and took upon Himself the full weight of human experience.

Creation Is Good

"And God saw everything that he had made, and behold, it was very good" (Gen. 1:31). God loves His creation. You may or may not. I may or may not. He has, after all, given us the freedom to disapprove of what He has done. But it should be noted with emphasis, God likes it! Since we are made in His image, we are probably in better rhythm and communion with Him when we are enjoying His creation than when we are continually shut up with our own problems in our air-conditioned offices, homes, and cars.

Many are restored by being at the beach; others by being in the bosom of a mountain. Nature, which is our term for God's creation here on earth, has restorative value for us. Sometimes it takes a day or two away from phone, television, and responsibilities before we begin to hear again the soft sounds of creation. When we begin to really hear them again, we generally find ourselves in close proximity with the presence of God.

> Drop thy still dews of quietness,
> Till all our strivings cease;
> Take from our souls the strain and stress,
> And let our ordered lives confess
> The beauty of thy peace.
>
> —John Greenleaf Whittier

God's Word Begins Any New Creation

The created order was spoken into being. Each new act of the Creator is accomplished by a word. With God's speech, the deed is done. The Hebrew word used here is the word *amar.* While it is used in many ways in the Old Testament, here it is used as direct command.

It speaks of God's power to speak into being, to command into being, if you please, that which once was not. Further it emphasizes His pledge to sustain what he has brought into being. It also serves as a *type* or shadow of that which is to come, that is, "the Word become flesh" (John 1:14). What is so intriguing is the incredible emphasis upon the word God speaks. The word envelopes both His pledge and His action. At the beginning of each new phase of creation, God's word is enough. Michelangelo's marvelous work in the Sistine Chapel portrays God reaching out with His finger to touch Adam. That is a marvelous painting and I would in no way detract from it. But the imagery of Genesis 1 is verbal. When it came that eternal moment to create, God spoke it into being. "And God said, 'Let there be light'; and there was light" (Gen. 1:3). "And God said. . . ." God's new beginnings are always accompanied by His word.

In the New Testament, we discover that the emphasis shifts to demonstrate more clearly that the creative word is also the redemptive Word. Always the Word creates new possibilities. That is true even of our words which are in response to His Word. Consider the word that is finally spoken by a penitent sinner who now experiences cleansing and newness of life. What of those words our Lord gave to the woman who had been caught in the act of her sin? "Neither do I condemn thee. Go, and sin no more." Saul of Tarsus heard a voice from heaven calling his name, words of new beginning that changed him from Saul to Paul, apostle to the Gentiles. John began his first letter with these unforgettable words: "That which was from the beginning, . . . which we have seen with our eyes, which we have looked upon and touched with our hands, concerning the word of life . . . that our joy may be complete" (1 John 1:1,4).

Man Is Made in the Image of God

When the text gets to the creation of man, it does not simply announce, "next came man." Instead we are given the most incredible heaven-sent model about man, one that has been like a magnetic pull away from the lower depths to which humankind can fall. "Let us make man in our image, in the image of God he created him; male and female he created them" (Gen. 1:26-27).

The meaning of "image" is interpreted variously. Whatever "image" means, it is protected in the Second Commandment: "You shall not make for yourself a graven image, or any likeness of anything that is in heaven above, or that is in the earth beneath, or that is in the water under the earth; you shall not bow down to them or serve them" (Ex. 20:4-5). God cannot be contained in any man-made likeness. Man is prohibited from image-making but God's freedom of expression is unlimited. This essential prohibition is given because of our tendency to reduce God to less than He is. Once the image of God is thought to have been captured in a sculpture, a painting, or even in a heroic figure, things begin to disintegrate rapidly. The poetry of Robert Frost says it well:

> Our worship, humor, conscientiousness
> Went long since to the dogs under the table.
> And served us right for having instituted
> Downward comparisons. As long on earth
> As our comparisons were stoutly upward
> With gods and angels, we were men at least,
> But little lower than the gods and angels.
> But once comparisons were yielded downward,
> Once we began to see our images
> Reflected in the mud and even dust,
> "Twas disillusion upon disillusion.
> We were lost piecemeal to the animals,
> Like people thrown out to delay the wolves.
> Nothing but fallibility was left us,
> And this day's work made even that seem doubtful.[7]

The truth is that when we have cut God down to our size we no longer need Him.

What the "image of God" in man means must include the following dimensions which come directly out of the biblical narrative. Image means that man is created to have relationship with God, to share with Him in the wonder of creation, and to communicate with Him in the living of his days. Image means that man is free to choose in a way the other parts of creation are not free to choose. The image means that man is to be creative after the example of the Creator. Image means that man lives with a lonesomeness for the eternal, a kind of homesickness for the Creator. As a fish is made for water, as a bird is made for the air, so man is made for eternity. Until the breath of eternity begins to blow through his being, man feels continually displaced, out of rhythm with the way things were meant to be.

Yet image also means that man is at home in the garden of God's world and is to tend to it, be trustee of it, and exercise supervision of it. God's instructions to Adam about having dominion over the rest of God's creation came in the same sentence. "Let us make man in our image, after our likeness; and let them have dominion over . . . all the earth" (Gen. 1:26). Image means that not only are we to bear heaven's reflection but also earth's responsibility. We are to be trustees of God's world. We are destined to learn about it, discover its processes, and delight in its wonders. In other words, from the beginning, man was to engage in science, agriculture, art, animal husbandry, and all other activities that relate to the discovery, delight, and supervision of God's world. Science and technology were part of God's plan from the beginning. Yet, in uprooting themselves from the Source of their existence, science and technology now threaten the very existence of the planet they sought to explore. Again, when man loses the conviction of being made in the image of the Creator, things deteriorate rapidly.

For the Christian, the full promise of what it means to be made in the image of God is portrayed in Jesus Christ, who is the "Image of the invisible God" (Col. 1:15). In Christ, the mystery of being made in the image of God becomes intelligible and reachable. Through Him, we begin to realize our potentials as sons and daughters made in His image.

The believer who first was inspired to write what we know as Genesis 1 did not see all that Christ revealed, of course. Had he done so there would have been no need of the Word made flesh who dwelt among us. But the Genesis writer saw enough to lay the foundation. When Christ came, He built upon foundations already solidly in existence. What was needed was the fleshing out of what was seen from the very beginning. Mankind was not meant to be a "naked ape" but a son or daughter of the living God.

Scientific Anticipation in Genesis 1

What should we call one who had a scientific vision of the nature of things before science ever came into being? He cannot rightly be called a scientist as we measure a scientist, although I have taken the liberty to call him a scientist in this discussion. But he is no mere product of his era either. Consider that he lived during an era when men worshiped the planets, various animals, and lived by myths about mammoth ocean creatures. The author of Genesis not only affirmed that God did the creating but also as he spelled out the process of creation he had a sense of appropriate orderliness.

Some Scientific Parallels

The basic progression which the account takes is roughly the same as given to us by modern science if one accepts the evidence gathered in support of the Big Bang theory. With prescientific words, the account follows the various stages that were involved in the way the world came to be as we know it.

For example, current scientific thought speaks of the Big Bang and of the incredible amount of light that would have been generated in that explosion. The Genesis account begins its praise of creation in the same dramatic way. "God said, 'Let there be light;' and there was light" (Gen. 1:3). In an earlier era, skeptics who misused the Scripture to reinforce their cynicism, were forever pointing out the folly of the Scripture saying that light was created on the first day and the sun on the fourth. But the latest in scientific thought now agrees that light did happen first.

Then, according to scientific thinking, a period of great settling took place and the planets began to cool. Our own world eventually could be differentiated between water and dry land (Gen. 1:9). Obviously, before the plants could grow, there had to be both water and earth.

Plants had to come before other life. "Let the earth put forth vegetation, plants yielding seed" (Gen. 1:11). The reason for this is well known. Plants provide the oxygen which makes animal and human life possible. This process is studied by science classes everywhere and is called photosynthesis. It is made possible by a unique chemical substance called chlorophyll. It utilizes sunlight to compose out of carbon dioxide and water the basic plant components and nutrients needed for plant life. Incidentally, no one has succeeded in duplicating its action in a test tube. In fact, only chlorophyll within living plants is able to utilize sunlight in this particular way.[8]

Creation Is Progressive

One of the remarkable insights of Genesis 1 is that creation took place in stages. It was progressive. It didn't happen all at once. Even if it is held that creation took place in six literal days, creation is still presented as proceeding from one stage to the other. Keep in mind this vision preceded the scientific era by thousands of years.

There was no human background for this kind of perception on the part of the writer of Genesis. The clear truth is that Genesis 1 anticipated the direction that later understandings would develop. How difficult this is! For instance, in 1938 President Roosevelt assembled the brightest scientists in America at the White House to help him prepare for the things he might have to adjust to in the future. Yet after three days of speculation, these men who supposedly had their hands on the scientific future of the nation failed to anticipate atomic power, radar, rockets, jet aircraft, computers, photocopying, and many of the things we take for granted less than fifty years later. Yet these words from Genesis 1, long before the most simple scientific understandings of our world were formulated, anticipated the direction science would propose. One of its remarkable visions is that creation takes places in stages.

This is not to say that the Genesis 1 account can be turned into a scientific treatise. It can't. "Firmament," for example, is not part of our world view. To the ancients, the firmament was a kind of solid dome spanning the heavens. Elihu said to Job: "Can you, like him, spread out the skies,/hard as a molten mirror?" (Job 37:18). A scientific worldview probably would also place the creation of vegetation after that of the sun rather than before it. But all that misses the point unless Genesis 1 is substituted for a scientific textbook. The grandeur of the Genesis 1 praise account is that it steps completely away from ancient patterns of thought and is in rhythm with the way in which science indicates our world came into being. Creation is orderly. It is predictable. It is progressive. Man is to have dominion over creation. He is to study it and exercise stewardship over it. Light came first. Vegetation preceded creatures. Animals preceded man. Fantastic! All from one who lived at the very edge of what we would call history and civilization. Praise God and praise the man whose spiritual sensitivities allowed the revelation to get through.

Summary

In summary, the first chapter of Genesis is one of those biblical writings which makes one pause in humble reverence, like 1 Corinthians 13, Luke 2, or John 3. It is remarkable not only in its proclamation but also in its anticipation. Its insights remain relevant these many centuries later.

Genesis 1 suffers from two extremes. The first is from religious people who mistakenly try to make it into a scientific text and, in so doing, try to refute the scientists they fear are trying to ruin their faith. The second are the scientists who have long since ceased to be amazed by anything other than their own experiments and could not care less what any Scripture has to say. The first group seem to want a world without science. The second seem to want a world without God. As the believer who wrote Genesis 1 has shown us, we need a world with both.

Also, we, who frequently brush against the limits of our own abilities, stand in reverent awe when we realize how incredible it is that Genesis 1 could have been written when it was. It may be the best evidence for the inspiration of the Scripture in all of the Bible.

Notes

1. James M. Houston, *I Believe in the Creator* (Grand Rapids: William B. Eerdmans Publishing Company, 1980), p. 64.
2. Ibid., p. 66.
3. Clifford D. Simak, *Wonder and Glory, The Story of the Universe* (New York: St. Martin's Press, 1969), p. 194.
4. Ibid.
5. Morton Kelsey, *Encounter with God* (Minneapolis: Bethany Fellowship, Inc., 1972), p. 242.
6. T. S. Eliot, *The Complete Poems and Plays, 1909-1950* New York: Harcourt, Brace & World, Inc., 1952), p. 56.
7. Robert Frost, "The White-Tailed Hornet," *Complete Poems of Robert Frost* (New York: Holt, Rinehart and Winston, 1964), pp. 361-362. Used by permission.
8. Edward Teller, *Energy from Heaven and Earth* (San Francisco: W. H. Freeman and Company, 1979), pp. 40-41.

5
Creation and Chance

In James A. Michener's novel, *Space,* one of the key personalities in the beginnings of America's space program is Stanley Mott. One night, while attending a seminar at the great telescope on Mount Wilson, he chanced to see an amazing photographic plate which showed one of the most distant of galaxies, a galaxy so recently discovered it had not been given a name, only a number. The galaxy was seen edge-on, a thin, beautiful sliver of innumerable stars. In the dead center, as in our own galaxy, was a gigantic ball of generating fire. Mott realized that when he studied this remarkable plate, he was being given a glimpse of the way our own galaxy would look from outer space.

Michener describes Mott's encounter with the galaxy in lyrical phrases.

> As photographed from earth, this epic galaxy, this poem of the heavens, stood at an angle of forty-five degrees from the horizontal, the most effective possible presentation as if an artist had positioned it for maximum effect . . . this collection of a hundred billion separate stars, perhaps two hundred billion, this unity, this diversity, this terrible fracturing violence, this serene loveliness, this image of mortality which was surely destined for flaming destruction, what did the thing itself signify?[1]

What indeed? While Mott is a fictitious character, Michener's description is apt. Which one of us has not, on occasion been overwhelmed by the immensity, the vastness, the incredible beauty of the heavens? Scientists and Christians alike should seek answers to the question: What is the significance of all of this?

When secularism and science team together, they have an immense effect upon young men and women who are influenced both by the environment in which they live and the teachers who guide them. Many students are committed to the search for truth. When the foundation for life is believed to have come about by chance, eventually the purpose and meaning of a person's life is questionable. This is where the rub comes. The question is no longer academic. It ripples down into the basic fabric of life's meaning. James McGuire in *The Dance of the Pilgrim* suggests that one characteristic of the novelists of our age is that "chance and absurdity rule human actions. What philosophers call 'reality' is really chaos. There are no real causes, only twitches and spasms, ludicrous and grinding."[2] The practical effects of discarding the vision of creation as a purposive action of the Creator is turning out a cynical, empty generation.

The Dogma According to Chance

Science, as we have seen, has come to the understanding that the universe began. Scientists are now having to deal seriously with the universe's origins. The answer of many scientists with a secular bent might be summarized like this. "The belief that all things were created by a Creator who cares about us was fine for another era. But it is clear now, given our scientific expertise and with all of the troubles in the world, that there is no God, no loving Father in heaven. The universe came into being by the most remote of chances. As large as the universe is, it is inevitable that, in the law of probabilities, life should occur and men should evolve." Sometimes the phrases "random chance" or "mere chance" are used. But chance is, by its nature, random. The word *mere* is inappropriate relating to chance since chance is simply chance. That would be like saying mere dawn. Dawn is dawn and covers everything it touches. In hundreds of different ways, the secular message or parts of it come across in classrooms, books, speeches, and science programs for television.

As we shall see, chance is a poor candidate for the originator of the universe. In fact, chance just postpones the problem. If indeed all things came into being in a random fashion when matter collided at the doorstep of creation, where did the matter come from?

What we are dealing with is a prejudiced mind-set. At the bottom line, science can no more prove that chance created the cosmos than they can prove that God created the universe. One is not more scientifically provable than the other. Many who have dealt with racial prejudice in life and ministries will recognize the similarities. Secularism is prejudiced against any kind of God talk and especially prejudiced against the thought of a Creator. What we are dealing with is the same kind of prejudice that exists in racism. No amount of reason is going to convince a racially biased person that another race is not inferior. A similar bias exists in secularism. The mind-set against believing in God as the Creator of all things is so strong that no amount of reason seems enough to alter the pattern.

The difference between science and secularism needs clarifying here. Secularism is a mind-set, an environmental climate, in which life is organized with a definite bias against any belief in God. Science, by contrast, is concerned with the observation and classification of facts and laws relating to life, the world we live in, and the universe. Secularism often uses science to buttress its own bias against God, and sometimes science finds the cultural climate of secularism to its liking. But science is not of necessity secular. When a scientist chooses a secular mind-set, he or she is making a philosophical choice not a scientific statement.

Scientific bias against religious experience is based largely upon the completely different ways in which faith and science legitimize themselves. Their methods of verification are different. Science verifies through procedures producing "hard facts." Faith is verified, on the other hand, by inner spiritual experiences which can't be tested, measured, or weighed. Of course, the same can be said of emotion and all relationships. Love it is said, makes the world go around. Maybe so. But it would be hard to compile "hard facts" to prove that one way or another. Methods of verification need to be appropriate to the area being investigated.

The weaknesses of the secular belief system have been largely ignored. One place to begin in thinking through these matters is to proceed to the bottom line as we would in evaluating a financial statement.

Two Choices

Both science and Scripture now agree: What now exists once was not. Something or Someone caused it to happen. The question is what or Who brought all things into being. In its simplest form, only two choices present themselves. Either the universe, with all of its beauty, mysteries, and power, came into being through the Creator or it came into being through chance. If one opts to believe that it makes more sense to believe the universe is the result of the Creator, then the next question is, What kind of Creator? The Christian answer to that is a Creator-Redeemer, the One revealed in Jesus Christ our Lord. But if one opts to believe that chance is the reason things are, one is suddenly faced with some very tough questions. Before we deal with these questions, we must set the stage by looking at the process we humans use to come to conclusions about things.

Since and Therefore

Someone might object at this point that other possibilities might exist than Creator or chance. Why not think in terms of options we don't even know about? That is just the point. It is part of the human situation that we think between the points of *since* and *therefore.* The most common tasks and the most sophisticated systems are built upon the relationship between *since* and *therefore.* A few illustrations will suffice. We might think: since it is 6:30 AM, therefore, I must get up and go to work. Since it is Christmas time, I must send out some Christmas cards. Since I drive fifty-five miles and hour, I can expect to arrive at 8:00. And so on and on. Science moves continually from the since, which comprise the finding and facts, to the therefore, which is the hypothesis. Often either the since or the therefore is not actually expressed. But the reality is always present somewhere in the background.

Beliefs are established with the determination of the since. The since may be because of a carefully thought out logical system. Or it may, and most often does, arise out of experience. The person bruised by life might say, "Since my mother died of cancer, I don't believe in God anymore." Another might have the same experience and say, "Since my faith in God is so real and vital in my life, even in my mother's death I found strength and comfort." The difference is not in the situation but in the *since* from which they began.

Insofar as the origins of the universe are concerned, as always we move from since to therefore. We dodge the issue by suggesting there may be a reality somewhere that does not live between these two polar words. In no area of life would we allow ourselves this option, for we would simply cease to function. If science or someone else comes up with an alternate to chance, it will be dealt with at the time it arises. But the new alternative will still be a since that moves toward a therefore.

Implications of the Since and Therefore

The difference between the since of chance and the since of the Creator is seen in the therefores that result. The therefore of the most devout Christians is that they communicate with One they believe to be the Creator. They discovered this relationship in commitment to Jesus Christ. In Christ and in Scripture, they discover that the One whom they follow as Savior and Lord is the same One they meet when they ponder the mysteries of the night sky. Their experience is unified in Christ the Lord. They feel loved and respond by returning that love. Their Christian experience brings a sense of belonging, of being in place, of knowing and of being known. If the question is raised how the God mighty enough to create the world would have time to even notice a single individual, Galileo's answer is appropriate. "The sun," he said, "which has all those planets revolving about it and dependent on it for their orderly functions can ripen a bunch of grapes as if it had nothing else in the world to do."[3] The witness of Christians the world over is that the presence of Christ dwells with them as if the Creator had nothing else in the world to do.

When we turn to the implications of chance, we are in another chamber altogether. If we are products of chance, we are accidents. We are orphans in an uncaring universe, meaningless specks in a vast expanse. This is in fact how many people feel. The image we are left with, if chance is the reason behind everything, is faceless. It has no name. It has no address. It has no touch, no feeling, no dream.

What we lose when we opt for chance is what Martin Buber called the *Thou*.[4] He used the word *Thou* to describe the highest possible reality of life and relationship. *Thou* is personal, caring, relational, and transcends the impersonalism of life. At the other end of the scale Buber placed *It*. To relate to the world or to another person as an *It* is to respond to them impersonally, as things. Persons are meant to be loved, as *Thous*. Things are meant to be used, as *Its*. We sense that to be the right order. When the roles are reversed so that one is seen to use people and love things, we usually object, especially if the someone used is us. Yet if chance is the origin of everything, the reversal of *Thou* with *It* would seem inevitable.

I remember a graduate student who, bruised by life, considered himself an atheist. Ventilation was needed on his part, acceptance on mine. Eventually the healing process had to deal with his rejection of

God. Incredibly bright, he innately knew what his rejection of God meant. Part of his fright and panic was born out the realization that if God were not, he really was alone in a vast uncaring universe. After we got by the stage of anger turned on belief, I suggested that for a while he fasten his attention on doubting chance as he doubted the reality of God. This is the well-known discipline of doubting one's doubts. In the following weeks, he began to carefully put his faith back together. The launching pad was to realize the real problems involved in making chance the first cause of all things. To these we will now direct our attention.

Chance as Maker of Heaven and Earth?

Let us keep our attention on the basic issue. Did the universe come into being because of chance? Would it be in the nature of chance to create? The approach has some real problems. Let us look at some of them.

Does Chance Create?

Is it possible that the universe as we know it was authored by chance? Consider that chance always derives from possibilities already in existence. Clearly, chance is not a creator. The appropriate word for chance, if there is one, is *calculation* not *creation.* In asking the difficult questions about the beginning of the universe, chance is a poor candidate to put forward as originator. It simply postpones the questions. It passes the buck. Since chance can't create, we are left right where we began. Who created the realities out of which chance operates? If the great chain reaction was begun by the chance collision of particles of matter, who created the matter. Who created the possibility of the collision?

Creation Ex Nihilo

Now is probably a good time to turn to a good solid theological phrase, ex nihilo. It means "out of nothing." Christian theology has, through the centuries, spoken of creation ex nihilo. This means that the created order as we know it came into being by the purposive act of God, and that creation occurred from nothing. The Creator, by creative powers available and known only to Him, set in motion the power that created the universe.

Actually some scientists have proposed an ex nihilo solution to the question of origins. Edmund Whittaker, a British physicist wrote a book on religion and astronomy called *The Beginning and End of the World.* In it he said, "There is no ground for supposing that matter and energy existed before and was suddenly galvanized into action. For what could distinguish that moment from all other moments in eternity?" Whittaker concluded, "It is simpler to postulate creation ex nihilo—Divine will constituting Nature from nothingness."[5] The British theorist Edward Milne dealt with the subject mathematically and concluded, "As to the first cause of the Universe, in the context of expansion, that is left for the reader to insert, but our picture is incomplete without Him."[6]

Chance and Power

In all of creation, *power* is a key word. Nothing exists without power. Our ability to take a step is made possible by many complex chemical reactions which transfer the power inherent in the food we eat into the work we do. If the present Big Bang theory of creation is correct, the cosmos as we know it began with an immense explosion. Unthinkable power was unleashed. Our galaxy has a billion stars in it and there are a billion galaxies. Try to figure in your wildest imagination what kind of power created the potential for each of those galaxies to exist.

Since power is so vital, how does chance relate to power? Chance as we know it, does not have any power. Power is not its category. It does not even have the power to manipulate the odds calculated. One way to look at chance in a more sophisticated way is in actuarial science. An actuary may be one who calculates insurance risks and probabilities for an insurance company. Without such persons and without such calculations, insurance companies would have no idea how to set the premiums they charge their customers. The computations the actuaries make are involved and complicated. Power, however, is not a category which fits them. It is like saying how straight is blue or how long is yellow. Some categories can't be shifted from one dimension of reality to another.

Chance does not create power but probabilities. Yet it is impossible to talk of creation in any sense at all without power. It is an irony that science, which deals with the many dimensions of created power, so often dodges the questions of the origin of that power. Certainly it cannot be chance. Chance can calculate the odds on the wheel of fortune, but it has no power to turn the wheel.

Chance and the Ought

That man carries around a sense of ought is a curious phenomenon. All around the world men and women have a sense of what they ought to be or be doing. Even criminals have codes of behavior. While the dimensions of that ought vary from culture to culture, the ought is a constant for people everywhere in the world. The existence of the ought has challenged the best in the thinkers. Immanuel Kant, the great philosopher of another era, based his moral philosophy on this phenomenon. A more practical treatment is *Mere Christianity* by C. S. Lewis.

To explain the universal ought on the basis of chance is impossible. Whatever chance is, it does not have a conscience. Oughts are not its domain any more than power is.

Chance and Personality

Creation moves toward personality. It also moves toward the creative side of personality. In creation's progression from the simple to the complex, from the lifeless to the life-giving, the eventual keystone is personality or personhood. It would stand to reason that Whoever or whatever is behind creation would have to be at least as complex and as creative as persons are.

Creative persons can create things, but things cannot create persons. We know of no instance where the opposite progression takes place. That is, an artist may creatively produce a painting, but that painting cannot produce an artist. Man may invent machines, but those machines do not invent man. Authors write books, not books authors. Musical compositions are created by composers, not vice versa.

In creativity, the one whose imagination is involved exercises a creativity on a lesser level of creation than he or she is. Even when medical science creates the replacement of human organs, the replacement does not have the possibility of reproducing a man.

Creation moves ever toward the personal and creative, exalting both. Chance moves ever toward the impersonal and calculating; it doesn't create. Chance is by its nature impersonal. The impersonal does not create the personal. How difficult it is to explain personality if one begins with chance. How much easier and how much more convincing to explain personality with a belief in a personal Creator.

Chance and Meaning

Man is a searcher for meaning. Other parts of creation do not ask the question as to the meaning of their lives. Man keeps poking around the embers of life, seeking to find a niche and purpose. There is within the mind of man a lingering voice, still and small, almost lost in the clash of noises, which keeps insisting that life was meant to have purpose. People dream dreams and seek to fulfill them. The goal-setting enterprise is a reflection of a larger pool which speaks of meaning and purpose. Motivation has no meaning unless, somewhere in the great beyond, there is a purposive plot going on, the feeling that what we do matters.

What happens to meaning, purpose, dreams, goals, and motivation if everything comes from a random source? Why do we even ask questions like, What is the purpose and meaning of my life? Persons were made for meaning like birds were made for the air and fish for the sea. If the universe is reasonable, would it not seem that our need for meaning would find its source even as the need of a fish for water may find its source? We find meaning when we find a personal guiding Heavenly Father. But chance cannot help us to any degree with the meaning of our lives. It is not the cradle of dreams.

Pain, Suffering, and Chance

One suspects that the tendency of some to affirm a world begun by chance is to solve the problem of a suffering and painful world. If all things came into being by mindless chance, then it would make sense that life would be painful and cruel. A later chapter deals with pain and suffering. For now it is enough to point out that solution by subtraction is seldom a good answer to anything. On the lowest level, murder is a solution by "getting rid of." Cain slew Abel because his brother was a problem for him. At the highest level, reason sometimes gravitates toward the easiest solution, which is generally solution by subtraction.

A young boy was handed a puzzle. It was a little square board with holes drilled in it. The trick was to move all of the pegs to a certain place without jumping over any. Every time he tried he wound up with a peg or two out of place. In frustration, he took one of the unfitting pegs and threw it on the floor. He was using the time-honored method of solution by subtraction.

The cheapest way out of any theological tight place is to discard something. For instance, if one can't understand how Jesus Christ could be both man and God, the easy solution is to simply discard either Jesus' deity or His humanity. Again, if one finds the Christian doctrine of the Trinity difficult to understand, an easy way out is to discard the entire doctrine. An even more sophisticated approach is to discard one of the Persons of the Trinity.

When it comes to pain and suffering, the easiest way out is solution by subtraction. One solution is to discard evil and pain, declaring them illusions. Another is to discard the involvement of God with the world. In this view, God created the world but is unrelated to it. A final solution is to remove God altogether and replace Him with chance. The trouble with discarding something or Someone that seems a liability is that something truly important is lost. It is something like cutting off one's nose to spite one's face. Chance doesn't really solve the problem of evil. Believing that chance is the reason behind everything doesn't make pain hurt less or suffering more palatable. All it does is to show that chance is an inadequate solution.

One thing is certain. We who believe in God as the Creator of heaven and earth have been wrongly accused of taking the simple solution to things. It is usually quite the opposite. Christian theology at its best is the stubborn determination not to arrive at solutions by an easy subtraction. Every time something vital will have been rejected. On the other hand, what is more simplistic than to suggest the world came into being by chance?

Summary

When we move God out of creation and put chance at the headwaters of the universe, we cannot hang a no-vacancy sign out in front of such an explanation. Vacancies exist all over the place. I will summarize them here.

1. Chance does not create; it always deals with existing realities.
2. Chance is no substitute for creation ex nihilo, creation out of nothing. For chance to exist, something must already be.
3. Chance is powerless. Since creation and power are virtually synonomous, chance doesn't fit. Chance can calculate but not energize.

4. Chance has no conscience and is useless to explain why people everywhere experience an "ought." Values, morals, and standards are outside the territory in which chance operates.
5. Chance is impersonal. Creation moves from the impersonal to the personal, from the simpler to the more complex. The impersonal cannot create that which is personal. The statue cannot create the sculptor.
6. Chance is meaningless. Human life calls for meaning and purpose. Without these we become not more human but less human.
7. Chance is an easy explanation for pain and suffering. But it is solution by subtraction. Nor does it solve the problem. Pain is still real. Chance provides no dynamic for interpreting its significance nor its ultimate overcoming.

We have seen that chance is a frail substitute for a Creator. Yet we may expect continued emphasis in this direction in the coming years. The secular society of which we are a part is seductive in many ways. Our thought patterns are gently moved away from what we know by experience, by belief, and sometimes what we perceive to be common sense.

Conclusion

The cosmos had a beginning. Both Scripture and science agree on that. As to its origins we have two choices. Either we believe that the universe was created by the purposive act of a Creator. Or we believe that the universe was created by chance. Believing in the God who creates is not always easy to explain. Especially is that true when we deal with pain and suffering. But replacing the Creator with chance raises implications which, in any other human situation, would be called nonsense.

Notes

1. James A. Michener, *Space* (New York: Random House, 1982), p. 274.

2. John David MaGuire, *The Dance of the Pilgrim* (New York: Association Press, 1967), p. 10.

3. Samuel H. Miller, *The Life of the Soul* (New York: Harper and Row, 1951), p. 69.

4. Martin Buber, *I and Thou* (New York: Scribner's & Sons, 1928).

5. Robert Jastrow, *God and Astronomers* (New York: W. W. Norton & Company, Inc., 1978), p. 111.

6. Ibid., p. 112.

6

The Creation of Man

Something draws us to our roots. Alex Haley's book *Roots* is a reflection of this. Municipal libraries are full of citizens who are trying to find out their ancestry by going through the records of yesteryear. We have an urge to investigate our family beginnings. On an even deeper level, something pulls us to seek our original beginnings. Secular viewpoints that see man as a cosmic accident leave us drifters, rootless, here without purpose. As any gardener can tell you, trees withstand storms because of their roots. Contemporary man stands exposed to the storms of modern times precisely because all of the secular images given him lead to a sense of rootlessness, devoid of depth in any eternal soil. The secular mind has jettisoned the biblical images and realities which provide the soil in which the roots of the soul find security and growth. It is refreshing to turn once again to the revelatory truths and corrective images of the Scripture.

Genesis 2 and 3

With Genesis 2:4 we have an interpretation of creation from another viewpoint. It spotlights man. If the first chapter took the nature of an orderly progression, the second takes us to the heights and depths of man's possibilities. The inspiring Spirit spoke these words through an incredibly gifted man. He saw. He perceived. He understood. By means of Scripture, he left a permanent deposit of truth for the ages. His images are precise and indispensable. They are like stars by which ships navigate. Refusing to heed these leads to confusion, even shipwreck.

Some feel that this account was written by the same person as the first and is simply the second part of what was begun in the first chapter. Others consider the second to have been authored by another person. In any case the second supplements the first. The two chapters are quite different. The vocabulary change is one of the first things noticed. Next, the reader will notice that man, in Genesis 2, is placed at the very beginning of creation, before vegetation, animals, and woman. You will recall that in Genesis 1 creation happens progressively in six days. In Genesis 2, only one day is mentioned, probably being symbolic of the whole period of creation. In the first, man and woman are created at the same time. In the second, Eve comes later.

The reason for this variety would seem to rest in the different purposes of the writers. The first account is like a hymn of praise to the Creator of all of the universe. Its uniqueness is an orderly progression which includes the entire cosmos. The second account is topical. Its main concern is the couple in the garden of Eden, their uniqueness from the rest of creation and what happened to them there. The larger universe is not mentioned. His main concern was how Adam and Eve came to be as they were and what forces forged their being. This early theologian knew that the primary concern of persons within every era would be with themselves. The larger universe had been covered. He turned his spotlight on mankind.

While the final answers to the puzzle of man are revealed in Jesus Christ, as seen in another chapter, the broad outlines of these pieces of the puzzle are given to us in Genesis 2 and 3. Under the inspiration of the Holy Spirit, this early theologian drew with bold strokes the understanding of mankind to which all of the rest of the Bible points.

Adam and Us

At the outset, let's realize we are not simply theorizing about what some ancient writer wrote. We are talking about us. Adam is not only a proper name for the first man, it is the Hebrew word for *man.* Throughout the Old Testament, the Hebrew word for *Adam* is used in the same sense as we would use the word *mankind.* It is clear that, when the second Genesis account introduces the word *Adam,* it meant not only to give a name to the first man but also to suggest that the picture of Adam is the picture of every man. The struggle of Adam is also our struggle.

The importance of this understanding can hardly be overstated. Too often we have treated the account of Adam's creation as if it were a tale told in antiquity and fit for nothing better than a place among biblical antiques. The story was Adam's. But it is also yours and mine. It is a story of our innocence, freedom, temptation, and fall. This is not a story that begins, *once upon a time.* Present is its tense, not past. Its implications are current. It is instructive to note that in Genesis 2:24, the coming together of Adam and Eve, the present tense is used. "Therefore a man leaves his father and his mother and cleaves to his wife, and they become one flesh."

What then does the Scripture say about Adam and us in Genesis 2 and 3?

Man as a Special Act of God's Creation

With an economy of words, the author sketched man as a special act of God's creation. "Then the Lord God formed man of dust from the ground, and breathed into his nostrils the breath of life; and man became a living being. And the Lord God planted a garden in Eden, in the east; and there he put the man whom he had formed" (Gen. 2:7-8). Whatever view one takes of the method God used to create the universe and man, the indispensible rock upon which a purposeful view of life is formed is the belief that God is behind man's creation and his uniqueness. Indeed, it is difficult to explain this uniqueness without working from the special activity of the Creator.

The Uniqueness of Man

The psalmist was awed by the creation of man. For instance in Psalm 8, David wrote of the grandeur of heaven and the mystery of man in the midst of creation.

> When I look at thy heavens, the work of thy fingers,
> the moon and the stars which thou hast established;
> what is man that thou art mindful of him,
> and the son of man that thou dost care for him?
> Yet thou hast made him little less than God,
> and dost crown him with glory and honor (vv. 3-5).

We are unique. We human beings race around, put our bodies through immense stress and pressures, are constantly on the move from one place to another. Yet in spite of speed and stress, we manage to outlive most inanimate things around us (consider how many trees die after twenty or thirty years) and virtually all moving creatures.

The mountains and the rocks survive, of course, and a few trees, tortoises, and buildings. But by comparison, we are the most marvelous physical, spiritual, psychological, and rational living beings that we know of. We may not be able to swim like fish or fly like birds or run as fast as the gazelle; but in accomplishment, durability, and longevity, there is no created being which can compare. We are, as David said, something special.

Partnership with God in Caring for His World

In early Babylonian texts about creation, man was created merely to relieve the gods of their hard labors. In these early versions of creation, man was seen as providing food for the gods.[1] In sharp contrast, the biblical writer put man at the pinnacle of creation and showed man to be an overseer of creation in behalf of God. "The Lord God took the man and put him in the garden of Eden to till it and keep it. The man gave names to all cattle, and to the birds of the air, and to every beast of the field" (Gen. 2:15,20).

God is a delegator. Man is the one to whom He has delegated the high and holy task of caring for His world, including the people in it. Man is not simply a usable and disposable commodity. He shares responsibility with God for His earth (Gen. 1:28). As we saw in Genesis 1, one dimension of the image of God in man is the stewardship for taking care of God's world. Both ideas appear in the same verse (Gen. 1:26). Genesis 2 affirms and underlines the same theme.

Partnership continues in the New Testament.—Partnership with God in caring for His world comes to full stature in the New Testament. Here the primary concern is for the world of persons. "Simon, son of John, do you love me?" Jesus asked Peter. Peter's affirmative reply received this command, "Tend my sheep" (John 21:16). "We are labourers together with God," said Paul to the Corinthian Christians (1 Cor. 3:9, KJV). The ones who are strong are to undertake a special spiritual responsibility for those who are weak (Gal. 6:1). Jesus called the rich man who thought only of himself a fool (Luke 12:20). In another parable, the rich man is condemned because he shared no responsibility for the beggar Lazarus, indeed, seemed not to have noticed that he existed (Luke 16:19).

Spiritual gifts are given as God's commitment to this partnership.—In the New Testament, our special place is confirmed by God's continuing act of creation within the believer's life through the giving of spiritual gifts. These spiritual gifts are diverse. No believer is given all of them, but each is given at least one of them. Two features of spiritual gifts are common to all. The source of the gifts is God, and the recipients of the gifts are to use their gifts for others. Thus the grace of God finds continual ways of expression: "As each has received a gift, employ it for one another, as good stewards of God's varied grace" (1 Pet. 4:10).

Only humans can be in partnership with God. Without an understanding of this partnership, man floats, drifts, and wonders why he is here. With this vision, he is called to discover, develop, and use his special abilities in behalf of God's world. Only of Christian believers does Paul's little statement at the end of Colossians make sense: "And say to Archippus, 'See that you fulfil the ministry which you have received in the Lord' " (4:17). Only of believers could it be written: "So we are ambassadors for Christ, God making his appeal through us" (2 Cor. 5:20). Part of the uniqueness of man is the divine-human partnership to which he is called.

Roots in Eternity

Our beginnings are wrapped in the purposes of God at creation. God breathed into us and created within us the potential for eternity. Within each of us there exists a realm of activity we call the spiritual. Our roots are earth planted, but they are also God planted. Terms like *new birth, conversion,* and *born again* testify to the eternal calling within man to find his roots in eternity and in God. These terms are not simply religious phrases and "churchy" words. They are reflections of a reality that exists beyond the chemical components that make up a human being. They speak to the inner and spiritual rootedness of man in God.

One way to sense the need of this spiritual rootedness is to see what happens when it is erased from life. If life is not balanced by the eternal Word, man has the potential to become more beastly than the beasts. When we hear someone say, "Its a jungle out there," or "Its a dog-eat-dog world," we are hearing echoes of a world sealed inside its self-made materialistic canyon. The call to relationship with God continues to echo through the corridors of the soul, but it is often shrugged off as primitive superstition. The Light which lightens every man (John 1:9) is ignored. The trade-off is observable on every hand. A sense of futility and despair develops. Man has cut himself off from his spiritual roots.

Without the balancing eternal Word, man tends to deny his stewardship for the world God created. It is hard to live with a sense of trusteeship for God's world when the world is no longer believed to be God's. It is our spiritual rootedness that works its way into concerns for the world, for others, for future generations. One reason we are in the environmental mess we are in is because we have lost the spiritual roots which have provided a conscience about the way in which God's world is to be treated. David's hymn of praise in Psalm 8 includes this dimension also. "Thou hast given him dominion over the works of thy hands;/thou hast put all things under his feet." (Ps. 8:6). One of the critical questions of our time is, What happens to our dominion over the earth when the vision of creation as the work of "thy hands" is ignored? All too often the answer is an ecological nightmare.

Through the sensitivities of faith, the believer senses that both he and the earth are parts of God's creation. A kind of inner resonance develops between nature, man, and God. Elizabeth Barrett Browning expressed the reality of this triangle when she wrote:

> Earth's crammed with heaven,
> And every common bush afire with God;
> And only he who sees takes off his shoes—
> The rest sit round it and pluck blackberries.

Creatures of the Dust

Yet, our uniqueness has limited dimensions to it. Adam is pictured from the first as unique, yet rooted to the earth from creation. "Then the Lord God formed man of dust from the ground" (Gen. 2:7). With vivid imagery, the writer summed up the origin of the earthly and heavenly possibilities in us all. God breathes into us His life. He forms us from the earth. We can be saintly. We can be beastly. From the beginning, we bore the terrain of this earth and all that was before us. We also bear the breath of God within. The sounds of eternity are not beyond our reach. Yet we often choose earthly ways. We allow ourselves to be squeezed into a worldly mold.

What that tough-minded theologian of Genesis has done is thrust upon us a rock-ribbed realism that understands both the earth from which we come and the spiritual heights to which we can attain. For those who object to the idea that we are kin to the apes, the Genesis account gives little solace: "Of dust from the ground!" (At least he could have said we are diamonds in the rough!) Descendants of the dirt? But he will not soften it. He will not allow us to miss his point. Man is not God, heavenly. He is man, earthly. He is not Creator, only creature. He may spend all of his life playing god, but the Genesis account snickers at his attempt. He may pamper his life as if he were the center of everything, but the Genesis writer knew he wasn't the center of anything. Not even his world is the center of anything. Only God is center. The psalmist knew it well.

> Before the mountains were brought forth,
> or ever thou hadst formed the earth and the world,
> from everlasting to everlasting, thou art God.
> Thou turnest man back to the dust,
> and sayest, "Turn back, O children of men!" (Ps. 90:2-3).

Still, the fact that we are creatures with the imprint of both earth and eternity upon us is hardly enough to explain the problems we seem capable of making for ourselves and our world. Some other factors must be involved. The Genesis account helps us to more fully account for the puzzle we are and the predicament we are in.

Realities of the Nature of Man

The realities within which we live our lives are drawn for us by the Genesis word. A definition of reality is in order. *A reality is something to which we must adjust. It will not adjust for us.* The realities, the bedrock truths, which the writer, through inspiration, saw from that early moment of history, are as sturdily set and unmovable for us as they were for him.

Boundaries

Boundaries are the laws, rules, and understandings by which and within which man lives. Boundaries provide stability in life. Without them, we would not long survive. What would happen if every new day laws were changed, boundaries were switched, and rules were altered? As we saw in the chapter on beginnings, man requires a large measure of stability.

The psalmist once reflected that "the boundary lines have fallen for me in pleasant places;/surely I have a delightful inheritance" (Ps. 16:6, NIV). He was reflecting on the lines within which he lived. These included the expectations, the surroundings, the heavenly tasks, and the earthly responsibilities. For the psalmist they had been pleasant, not cruel. Adam might have said the same thing. He had been delegated responsibility by the Creator to tend the garden. After God created the other creatures he brought them to Adam to be named. Nor did God edit out the ones He didn't like. "Whatever the man called every living creature, that was its name" (Gen. 2:19). That was an important and rewarding task for Adam. The boundary lines had been pleasant. But there was this tree. . . .

Is the moral law a "real" boundary?—God set a boundary for Adam. This one was a moral boundary. Moral boundaries have three characteristics. They are spoken into being by God. Eventually dire consequences develop if they are transgressed. Also involved is the freedom to choose. Adam and Eve faced for the first time the reality that they could put something else besides God as center of their garden, their world. They could put their own choices. "You may freely eat of every tree of the garden; but of the tree of the knowledge of good and evil you shall not eat, for in the day that you eat of it you shall die" (vv. 16-17). Implicit in the command given to Adam was the judgment that would follow if the boundary were transgressed. "For in the day that you eat of it you shall die" (v. 17). They did not, after their sin, breathe their last. But something died within them and their world. Judgment came to fruition in their final deaths.

When God was replaced as center by that which He had created, the world experienced something dreadful that theologians have called "the fall." The fall was no small thing. It was, at its heart, the enthroning of the created self as god. Adam and Eve wanted to be like God. They wanted control. The serene innocence of the garden was suddenly brought to a screeching halt. God was replaced by a new landlord, by a new king and queen. The tender moral balances were tilted by the addition of a new center. The created had chosen to usurp the position of the Creator.

Our concern here is with the boundaries built into our very beings. God set Adam's boundary. Sometimes we call these moral laws. Moral laws, such as the Ten Commandments, are not given to persecute the happiness of man but to provide for his stability and survival.

We live in an era that questions whether any absolute boundaries, or any absolute moral laws, exist. Elton Trueblood points out that this is a new situation. "Always men have broken laws; that is nothing new. What is new is the acceptance of a creed to the effect that there really is no objective truth about what human conduct ought to be. The new position is not merely that the old laws do not apply, but rather that *any* moral law is limited to subjective reference."[2]

Whether there is a stubborn reality called the moral law which exists within man is a vital question. If there are no real boundaries, there are no transgressions. And if there are no transgressions, there is no such thing as being lost. Which means there is no such thing as being found.

Part of our problem is that we haven't made distinctions between that which is arbitary and that which is built into man by God from the beginning. Dorothy Sayres, in her book *The Mind of the Maker,* thinks through these in a careful and helpful way by making distinctions between physical laws, moral laws, and religious codes.[3]

Some would assume that all moral laws are arbitrary, reflecting either someone's bias or background. This is why so many believe there are no moral absolutes. "Everything is relative," is the way it is sometimes expressed, a statement which is itself a contradiction. Obviously, "everything is relative" is an absolute statement. But of course, everything is not relative. For instance the laws of physics are not relative but utterly predictable. Moral laws aren't relative either. Now it is true that much legislation expresses little more than individual preferences. They are necessary but they are neither absolute nor universal. Whether we drive on the left side of the road as in England or the right side as in America is not a moral law but a preference. There is a world of difference between a law which says, "Thou shalt not drive on the right side of the road," and one which says, "Thou shalt not murder."

Adam's transgression of the boundary God set is not only his story but also our story. Moral law is there. We may think for a time that the boundary has adjusted itself to our choosing or our behavior. But eventually we discover, as did Adam, that it didn't move because we moved. History tends to underline this truth as well. The Hitlers and the Stalins have their day, but God is still God, and moral boundaries are still in place. Time will expose that the moral hinge around which things turn is still in place. The first reality which the early writer saw was that we all live within boundaries placed by the Creator. Stepping outside of these does not erase them. When we quibble with them, we reflect that Adam's story is indeed our's.

Relationships

The second great reality of life is relational. Relationships provide us with the security to learn how to love. Without healthy relationships, man is never secure. Without security, love in any mature sense is impossible. With this in mind, God created man for relationship, not solitary existence. "Then the Lord God said, 'It is not good that the man should be alone' " (2:18). The degree to which we are intimate as human beings varies. That we are relational beings does not. We were conceived by means of a relationship. Without the help of others, we would not survive. That is why God gives us a family. When we are old enough to get about on our own, even if the family of which we are part does serve as trustee for our welfare, we still seek out others. Even juvenile delinquents often travel in gangs.

Relationships are vertical and horizontal.—Adam's relationship with God was seen from the beginning to be inadequate in and of itself. Adam already had a relationship with God and already had received the commandment about the tree in the garden when it was written: "Then the Lord God said, 'It is not good that the man should be alone.' " Thus the relationships around which Adam's life would turn were both horizontal and vertical, with Eve and others later and with God. All biblical teachings rest upon these two relational dimensions which were in place from the beginning: the vertical with God, the horizontal with man. Consider this teaching of Jesus.

> "Teacher, which is the great commandment in the law?" And he said to him, "You shall love the Lord your God with all your heart, and with all your soul, and with all your mind. This is the great and first commandment. And the second is like it, You shall love your neighbor as yourself. On these two commandments depend all the law and the prophets" (Matt. 22:36-40).

In contemporary life, the importance of the human side of relationships is widely recognized. Psychology and sociology both speak to the need for healthy interpersonal relationships. When an individual, from early childhood, is deprived of love and care, the deprivation is carried into adulthood. This has given rise to a whole sector of our society which devotes itself to the healing of fractured relationships. The need for human relationship was perceived and revealed from the earliest Genesis accounts. With all of our technology, we have not moved beyond, "It is not good that the man should be alone."

Sin breaks relationships.—Adam's relationship with God remained untested until Adam transgressed the boundary which God set for him. Then the relationship was rent. The picture of Adam after his sin is a picture of alienation from the One upon whom he depended. Adam hid. He was ashamed. He put the blame on Eve, who, in turn, put the blame on the serpent. But God took the initiative in seeking to restore the severed relationships. God broke the silence of separation: "But the Lord God called to the man, and said to him, 'Where are you?' " (Gen. 3:9). Even the transgression had not erased the basic design of God to relate to man and to enjoy a daily partnership with him.

Freedom

The third leg of reality portrayed in the Genesis account is that of freedom. Freedom fuels for man the possibilities of life. In the soil of freedom, love, trust, and joy grow. Without freedom, the thrill of discovery and the adventure of faith would be gone. If we did not have the freedom to choose who will be our friends, what we will do, and whom we will love, we would feel trapped. Like so many other essentials of life, we don't appreciate it enough because we've seldom had to do without it.

Freedom from the biblical point of view is a sheer gift of God. God willed that man should have a will. God chose that man should be able to choose. The choosings would be severely limited. Indeed, through the centuries the arguments have waged whether man has any freedom at all. It used to be waged within the boundaries of religion. Now it is also being waged in the boundaries of psychology. But even the fact that we can argue about whether we have it would indicate that we do.

Allowing freedom is risky business.—What awesome risks God decided to take in that pristine moment of eternity when He willed for man a will. For within that gift of freedom, man can do that which is incredibly beautiful and that which is hideous. He can be creative and cruel. Through freedom, we become capable of not only great good but also great evil. We are creative by our very natures, yet seem to destroy as much as we create. There is probably not a habitable sector of our globe that has not been argued about, fought over, and the boundaries moved. We hate as much as we love and divide as much as we unify. We are victims of the wrath of others and spreaders of scars ourselves. With the nuclear age, we now have the potential to destroy ourselves and our posterity.

The dreadful and beautiful part of freedom is that it allows. It decides to limit control. The allowances of God with man may be understood in a tiny way when any parent begins to allow the child more freedom. The most scary of all is when the driver's license is obtained! When God decided for freedom, He decided to give up some of the controls, just as a parent decides the same for a child. When Jesus called God *Father,* He was suggesting that we try to understand our relationship with God as a parent and a child. As earthly parents, we begin to empathize with God when we realize the risks He took in willing for all of us a will and allowing us the freedom to choose.

How much freedom is the right amount?—Did God give us too much freedom? It depends upon what His goal was. If His goal were a tidy, sterile, unmessy world, then He gave us too much. But if He desired sons and daughters to love, if He wanted us to be creative, if He wanted us to grow, if He wanted us to develop responsibly, then He had no other choice of which we are aware. For the soil in which all of these grow is called freedom. We can begin to understand where God was at the moment of creation when we are called upon to make the same decision in granting freedom to our children. It is a trade-off. Too much control and the casualties are obvious: creativity, love, growth, and responsibility. Too much freedom and the possibility of self-destruction results.

God's decision, observable from our human vantage point, was to give structured freedom. In so many ways our lives are determined. We do not have a choice of parents, of bodily construction, of race, mother language, or sex. Parents, culture, and educational and economic background all determine our lives more than we want to admit. We even build limited freedom into our organizations and institutions to keep things from falling into chaos. Sometimes too much structure develops and too little freedom. But structures and systems are a major part of the human way of doing things. They serve as a kind of a ratchet to keep things from falling apart or backwards.

Still that beautiful grace of freedom which is God's gift to us by creation determines so much of what we become. We do choose our beliefs, our relationships, our attitudes in the midst of adversity, our values, and, in many ways, our behavior. We can, and do, change. As the atom has taught us, it doesn't take much to exert great power. So it is that freedom exerts immense power both for good and for evil.

Adam chose. He chose wrongly and was driven from his innocence. In all of the debates about how Adam's sin affects the rest of us, we tend to overlook the basic grace of it all. God took the risk to give Adam the right to choose, even wrongly.

The Voices that Influence

A final reality within which man must live is that he is influenced by many voices. He is not a simple creature, simply responding to instinctive forces within. He is complex, with many voices demanding his attention and allegiance.

The first voice is God's.—From the beginning, God spoke the worlds into being. His very nature is to communicate. In the Old Testament, God is pictured as One who loves to communicate with His creation, even if it is in argumentation. "Put me in remembrance, let us argue together;/set forth your case, that you may be proved right" (Isa. 43:26). God is troubled by our silence. For no relationship can long endure without reinforcement. The relationship between God and man, just as the relationship within marriage and family, needs nourishment. As C. S. Lewis says, "The worst we have done to God is to leave Him alone."[4]

The second voice is from the serpent.—Evil, housed in this instance in the serpent, had its own say. The tempter's line was effective, if predictable. The serpent cast doubt on the boundary God had set and upon the trustworthiness of God Himself. Most of all, it suggested that a whole unrealized world existed for Adam and Eve to experience.

When the devil came to tempt Christ in the wilderness, he came talking. He offered an open door for the Messiah to walk through: "All these I will give you if you will fall down and worship me" (Matt. 4:9). Unlike the first Adam, the last Adam (which is what the New Testament sometimes calls Jesus, see 1 Cor. 15:45) didn't choose to take Satan up on his offer. "Begone, Satan! for it is written,/'You shall worship the Lord your God/and him only shall you serve' " (Matt. 4:10). It is important to remember that Satan is a smooth talker, a good salesman, and he knows how to close the sale.

The third voice is from Eve.—Other people influence us also, especially those who are called "meaningful others." These are the people upon whom we depend for meaning and significance in life. They may be right, or they may be wrong; but we carefully consider what they say. This is one reason it is so important to choose our close friends carefully. Jesus had friends among all classes of people, but when He went to Gethsemane, He took only the twelve (excluding Judas) and finally, only Peter, James, and John. They didn't help. They slept. But the fact that the Lord needed them is instructive to all of us. We need others and their encouragement.

The final voices came from within Adam himself.—These voices are not recorded in Genesis. Neither are our inner voices recorded for others to tune in on. Aren't we glad! What a confused mumbo jumbo it would sometimes be. Sometimes it would be embarrassing.

One can almost sense the tug and pull of the inner voices of Adam and Eve in that garden moment. There was a real division in what has been called "the parliament of the person." The apostle Paul knew it well. To express this division from within, he used the words *flesh* and *spirit.* The one side he called the flesh. Works which resulted from listening to this voice are not those used in hymnals: immorality, impurity, licentiousness, idolatry, sorcery, enmity, strife, jealousy, anger, selfishness, dissension, party spirit, envy, drunkenness, carousing, and the like (Gal. 5:19-21). The positive side he described as the Spirit. "The fruit of the Spirit is love, joy, peace, patience, kindness, goodness, faithfulness, gentleness, self-control; against such there is no law" (vv. 22-23). Spiritual maturity learns to discern the voices and the works that they produce.

The Intrusion of Evil

The intrusion of evil on the scenes deserves our special attention. The serpent embodies evil in the garden story. Evil was not part of the nature of man from the beginning, for in their innocence Adam and Eve lived without shame. Shame is the earliest indicator that innocence had fled. Evil is an outside influence upon man. It is not part of the physical, emotional, or rational dimensions of man. It appears on the scene when freedom arrives. What is the nature of this outside intrusion in life?

Evil Is a Secondary Power

Evil is not a primary power in the story of creation. It is not a creator. It is a parasite, living off of that which has already been created. It cannot create that which it feeds upon. It cannot bring into being that which it influences. Some overestimate its power and fear it is equal to God's creative work in our behalf. Some underestimate its power and do not realize the destruction evil can bring about.

The main strategy of evil is to manipulate freedom and use it to violate boundaries and relationships. The serpent manipulated Adam and Eve. He did not speak the truth but was so believable. Adam and Eve became true believers. As can be observed in all of life, the first casualty was the boundary God put before them. The second was their relationship with Him. These two are the first to go whether we are talking about a war or the breakup of a marriage. These are constants, and the Genesis writer saw it all clearly from the beginning.

Evil in Today's World

For this early theologian, evil was a reality, an independent reality which existed apart from Adam and Eve and sought to destroy God's purposes for them, not open to debate. Twentieth-century man has often adopted a curious attitude toward evil. In spite of two world wars, the extermination of six million Jews in the Second World War, the exploitation of people and environment, the rise of international terrorism, and the threat of nuclear destruction, many would question the existence of evil as an independent reality over and beyond ignorance and superstition. An exception to this is a study done by psychiatrist M. Scott Peck in his book, *People of the Lie.* Peck described the experiences and studies which have brought him to his present conclusions about evil. Of interest to me, who profited greatly from his earlier book *The Road Less Traveled,* was this sentence from his later work about evil. "I referred earlier to Jesus as my Lord. After many years of vague identification with Buddhist and Islamic mysticism, I ultimately made a firm Christian commitment, signified by my . . . baptism on the ninth of March 1980, at the age of forty-three—long after I had begun working on this book. . . . My commitment to Christianity is the most important thing in my life and is, I hope, pervasive and total."[5]

Later in a chapter entitled "Toward a Psychology of Evil," Peck wrote:

> Bear in mind also that just as the issue of evil inevitably raises the question of the devil, so the inextricable issue of goodness raises the

question of God and creation. While we can—and, I believe, should—bite off little pieces of mystery upon which to gnash our scientific teeth, we are approaching matters vast and magnificent beyond our comprehension. Whether we know it or not, we are literally treading upon holy ground. A sense of awe is quite befitting. In the face of such holy mystery it is best we remember to walk with the kind of care that is born both of fear and love.[6]

The Origin of Evil

Since there is a reality we call evil, where did it (or he) come from? Evil exists over and beyond the atoms and molecules of nature, the foibles and flaws of mankind, just as God does. From whence then does it come? The answer is quite simple; we do not know. This may be why so many reject evil as an independent reality. It is hard to accept that there are some things we just do not know and are not going to find out. But to reject a reality because we do not know its origins is foolish. That is like refusing to watch television because we do not know who made the set. Thinkers through the ages have toyed with the origins of evil. Some of these speculations are thought to be in the Bible, but they are not. The Scripture simply does not tell us other than emphasizing that God is the ultimate source of all (Gen. 3:1). The Genesis account ignores the question completely. The serpent suddenly appears with no explanation of how he got there.[7]

Some try to resolve the problem by simply creating two equal forces, one divine and the other demonic. This is called dualism. But dualism finally breaks down and calls for something over and beyond the two realities to be "the whole show." The biblical witness is that God created all things. This includes the possibility that evil would arise and manipulate the freedom Adam and Eve had been given in the garden.

Some suggest that evil may be a by-product of the granting of freedom to Adam and Eve. Does evil as well as good grow from the soil of freedom, the freedom which is the gift of God? James M. Houston sees this possibility.

> The biblical story is not concerned, then, with the origin of evil so much as the beginning of man's responsibility. The origin of evil is lost in a wider mystery of freedom for man to choose, and to be responsible. . . . God has accepted the terrible, awesome implications of evil within

His creation, as the responsibility only God can take and for which only He can provide a remedy.

Perhaps we do best to handle it like the apostle Paul did. He knew all too well its reality: "For we are not contending against flesh and blood, but against the principalities, against the powers, against the world rulers of this present darkness, against the spiritual hosts of wickedness in the heavenly places" (Eph. 6:12). As to its origins, he was content to speak of the "mystery of iniquity" (2 Thess. 2:7, KJV). This much we do know. In the Genesis account, certain things—relationships, boundaries, and the freedom to choose—are in place before evil appears as an independent reality apart from Adam and Eve.

The Nature of Evil

The Genesis account is not concerned with the origin of evil but its nature. The writer unmasks the nature of evil for us.

Evil is experienced personally.—Adam and Eve did not deal with some impersonal force, such as the law of gravity. They dealt with a personal reality who knew them and exploited them individually. "Did God say, 'You shall not eat of any tree of the garden?' But the serpent said to the woman, 'You will not die. For God knows that when you eat of it your eyes will be opened, and you will be like God, knowing good and evil' " (Gen. 3:1,4). The tendency of our age to prefer the impersonal has led many to depersonalize evil, turning it into an intangible force or impersonal power. The Scripture disagrees with this approach and stays with the personal dimensions from beginning to end. Whether the name given to this reality we experience personally is the devil, or Satan, the personal dimension is never erased. To make evil impersonal may make it more palatable for the modern mind. It may also leave us more exposed.

Evil exploits our weak points.—When Satan suggested to Eve that "you will be like God," bingo, he hit pay dirt. To be like God, or to play god is an ever present temptation. The more success realized, the greater the temptation to assume Godlike proportions in wealth, reputation, popularity, or religion. C. S. Lewis penetrated the situation precisely. "From the moment a creature becomes aware of God as God and of itself as self, the terrible alternative of choosing God or self for the centre is opened to it. This sin is committed daily by young children and ignorant peasants as well as by sophisticated persons. . . . We try, when we wake, to lay the new day at God's feet; before we have finished shaving, it becomes *our* day and God's share in it is felt as a tribute which we must pay out of 'our own' pocket, a deduction from the time which ought, we feel, to be 'our own.' "[8]

Part of the subtlety of Satan is that he knows religious language. We who are thought by others to be religious do well to remember that. James pointed out to the first-century Christians that "even the demons believe—and shudder" (Jas. 2:19). When Satan comes to church, and his favorite time is Sunday, we may be sure he is not going to be using the language of the gutter. We are, in truth, defenseless against him without Christ. Martin Luther understood this as few Christians have.

> Did we in our own strength confide,
> Our striving would be losing;
> Were not the right Man on our side,
> The Man of God's own choosing;
> Dost ask who that may be?
> Christ Jesus it is he;
> Lord Sabaoth, his name,
> From age to age the same,
> And he must win the battle.

Evil keeps some constant companions.—Wherever evil goes, and that covers the landscape, constant companions are the same as Adam and Eve experienced in the garden. Guilt is one. Shame is another. Add to that hiding or deceit. Finally, there is projecting the blame on others.

Adam and Eve wound up with a good case of all these. Special mention needs to be made of guilt. It is a constant companion to many. We need to make a distinction between true guilt and false guilt. False guilt is when we don't measure up to some arbitrary expectation, such as not being as smart as our sisters. False guilt leads to inferiority. Real guilt, or guilt from violating a moral boundary, brings those companions of evil already listed: shame, hiding, and blaming someone else. This story line is observable in most of the literature and drama of our era. One trend is to do away with shame. The thought is that, in doing away with shame, we will have done away with some nuisance long regretted. This is a little like pulling the Trojan horse inside the walls of Troy and celebrating the event. "The frankness of people sunk below shame is a very cheap frankness."[9]

God's Initiative

God took the initiative in seeking to reestablish the relationship between Himself and man. But things are never the same. Adam and Eve could never return to the innocence from which they came. Nor can we. Eden's gate was shut to them. It is to us also. Modern attempts to solve man's problems by a return to "being natural" are doomed to failure precisely because we can't return to innocence. There is no way back, only a way through, that is the way through redemption in Jesus Christ, God's final initiative in our behalf. The Creator must become Redeemer. As we shall see, He knew that "before the foundation of the world."

Notes

1. James M. Houston, *I Believe in the Creator* (Grand Rapids: William B. Eerdmans Publishing Company, 1980), p. 66.
2. Elton Trueblood, *A Place to Stand* (New York: Harper and Row, 1969), p. 15.
3. Dorothy L. Sayers, *The Mind of the Maker* (New York: Living Age Books, 1958), pp. 19-30.
4. C.S. Lewis, *The Problem of Pain* (London: Geoffrey Bles, 1943), p. 45.
5. M. Scott Peck, *People of the Lie* (New York: Simon and Schuster, 1983), p. 11.
6. Ibid., p. 42.
7. Houston, pp. 87, 88.
8. Lewis, p. 63.
9. Ibid., p. 45.

7

Evolution as Process

Few issues have been more controversial for Christian belief than evolution and creation. Evolution comes from the Latin word *evolutio* which means an unrolling. Hence, evolution means an unfolding, a process of opening out, a changing. Biologically it is the word popularized by scientists during the last century who sought to explain the process by which any living organism has acquired the characteristics which distinguish it. Underline the word *process.*

When evolution broke with full fury on the human scene, it was a theory about a process. So it remained for several decades. In recent years, this has been subtly changing. With the realization that the universe had a beginning, some began to infer that chance and evolution were the two forces which brought the world to its present state. Evolution was thus elevated from process to designer or maker. The distinction between the process and the maker is thus blurred or dissolved altogether.

An illustration might help. Consider the cook in the kitchen and at the stove. In the process of preparing the meal the cook could be involved in several processes by which different foods are prepared. Later at the table the participants might discuss, even argue, about which process was used to prepare which dish. Recipes could be guessed at. The discussion could center on how the meal got there. All would understand that a cook was involved in these options.

The furor over evolution was earlier like this. The discussion centered around how creation got here. But it was understood that behind the "how" was a "who." Now suppose suddenly somebody began to argue that there was never anybody in the kitchen. The way in which the meal came to be could be completely explained by the processes involved. The "how" has now become the "who." That is the situation with evolution in much of today's thinking. What this means is that the Christian really has to deal with evolution in two ways, as process and as cause. In this chapter, we will look at evolution as a process. In the next, we will examine evolution as maker or designer.

To get into the subject, a little history of the controversy will help to bring us up to date.

Background of the Controversy

The most popular and influential of the scientists who first proposed the evolutionary theory was Charles Darwin. With the publication of *On the Origin of Species,* the controversey began in earnest.

Charles R. Darwin

Darwin earlier thought of entering the ministry and was encouraged by his father to do so. But his interest in the outdoors and natural phenomenon turned his attention to the natural sciences. The most important single influence in his life was a five-year trip around the world, during which he searched for fossils and studied plants, animals, and geology. After the trip he began formulating the theories which later aroused such great controversy. His theories suggested a process by which various types of animals and plants have their origin in other pre-existing types. Darwin suggested that the subsequent differences were due to modifications in successive generations. These modifications were thought to come about by natural selection, survival of the fittest, and sexual selection.

Darwin was convinced that he was onto something very significant. He also understood his limitations. In the preface to his book *The Descent of Man,* he stated: "My conviction of the power of sexual selection remains unshaken; but it is probable, or almost certain, that several of my conclusions will hereafter be found erroneous; this can hardly fail to be the case in the first treatment of a subject."[1]

Reading his journals, it can be concluded that Darwin believed in God, but not the scriptural view of a God who was intimately involved in the creative process. To use current jargon, his belief was that God programmed into creation the processes and possibilities observable in evolution and then let it run its course. In his current novel on Darwin, Irving Stone creates a fictitious conversation in which Darwin's wife Emma, who was a deeply religious woman, asked Darwin:

"Are you suggesting that there is no God?"

"I am suggesting that God, in the beginning, created certain laws. Then he retired, allowing His laws to work themselves out."[2]

A study of his letters and papers would suggest this to be an adequate statement of Darwin's belief. This is a form of Deism, which is the belief in God as Creator and final Judge, but, in the meantime, removed from the human scene and beyond the reach of human experience. It would reject the Christian doctrine of the incarnation, that God entered the human scene in Jesus Christ. Of interest, some of Darwin's greatest admirers were clergymen; some of his greatest enemies were clergymen.

Evidences Offered for Evolution

As evolutionary theory developed, it came to be based upon four mainstreams of evidence.[3] The first evidence given is *fossils.* Fossils are the remains or traces of things that lived long ago. They are preserved in rock layers called strata. When fossils in one layer differ from those of another layer, comparisons can be made between them. It is thought that these comparisons reveal the development of a form of life from one stage to another.

The second evidence offered for evolution is *embryology.* Evolutionary theory suggests that mammals are the last stage in a long evolutionary series of developments. The theory is that unborn mammals go through the same stages of development which groups passed through ages ago.

The third evidence offered is *comparative anatomy.* Comparisons are made between ancient animals' fossils, found in geological strata and current living things. The theory is that they must have a common source somewhere back in evolutionary beginnings. Attempts to find these beginnings and trace their developments is done by studies of fossils. Comparative anatomy is also used to explain the origin of structures within living creatures which are now useless. One's appendix is thought to be an example of this.

A final evidence presented by evolutionists is that of *geographic distribution.* Much evidence for evolution is thought to exist from plants and animals that live on islands far from continents. For example, Darwin made famous the Galapagos Islands which lie about six hundred miles from South America. Cut off from the mainland, some species of birds, lizards, and tortoises are quite different from those on the mainland. The theory is that they developed there because of changes that took place after their ancestors drifted from the mainland of South America.

Christians and Their Approaches to Evolution

Christian responses to evolution have covered the spectrum. On one end is the creationist movement which has opposed evolution vigorously throughout this century. On the other end are those who have embraced evolution as the primary way in which God has worked and continues to work within His world. Other viewpoints are tilted toward one or other of these extremes. Limitations of space will permit only a summary of these extremes.

Creationism and Evolution

Creationism is a term that has been taken over by a certain group who are in total opposition to evolution. Evolution is thought to be a major threat to the biblical account of creation. Opposition to it has been sustained since the beginning of this century.

Early creationist efforts centered in great personalities.—The beginning of fundamentalist opposition centered in William Bell Riley (1861-1947). Riley was pastor of the First Baptist Church, Minneapolis, Minnesota. In 1919 he was instrumental in founding the World's Christian Fundamentals Association, a group of churches bound together by their premillenial and dispensational understanding of the Scripture. Riley did, however, believe that the days of Genesis 1 were ages, believing that the testimony of geology necessitated this approach. The Scofield Reference Bible, in its later editions, interpreted the days of creation in Genesis as long periods of time also.

The famous Scopes trial in Tennessee pushed William Jennings Bryan to the forefront of the evolutionary debate. Secretary of state under Woodrow Wilson, Bryan was a Presbyterian layman who suffered greatly from the stress of the trial. Although Scopes was found guilty of teaching evolution in a state which prohibited such, Bryan never recovered. He died shortly thereafter.

Harry Rimmer was an eloquent spokesman against evolution. He spoke with the authority of a minister, which he was (Presbyterian), and a research scientist, which was questionable. His laboratory was a small one in the back of his house. He eventually joined W. B. Riley's Christian Fundamentals Association as a field secretary and lecturer.

George McCready Price wrote the text for early antievolution forces. A Seventh-Day Adventist, who served as principal in a small high school in Eastern Canada, he was greatly influenced by the vision of Seventh-Day Adventist prophetess Ellen G. White. She claimed divine inspiration for a vision of a universal flood which accounted for the fossil record of geology. Evolutionary theory was thought to be based largely upon this fossil evidence.

Price began to read everything he could get his hands on concerning evolution. He authored several books attacking evolution, particularly its geological foundation. Eventually his *The New Geology* became the standard text for fundamentalists in their opposition to evolution. In it Price thought he had proved that there was no natural order to the fossil-bearing rocks, all of which he attributed to the Genesis Flood. Harry Rimmer called it "a masterpiece of REAL science."[4] Another viewpoint was held by David Starr Jordan, president of Stanford University, an authority on fossil fish. "It would be just as easy and just as plausible and just as convincing if one should take the facts of European history and attempt to show that all the various events were simultaneous."[5]

Early efforts of fundamentalism in the fight against evolution were afflicted with two great weaknesses. The first was lack of agreement on just what they were proposing. Riley and Bryan both believed that the days of Genesis were geological ages. Price insisted that the six days of creation were literal twenty-four-hour days. Rimmer, on the other hand, favored two separate creations. The first he said happened millions of years ago and was covered in the opening words, "In the beginning." The second, approximately four thousand years before Christ, happened in six literal days. Price insisted upon a universal flood. Rimmer believed in a local flood. Nor were they always kind to each other. Price labeled W. B. Riley's interpretation of a Genesis day as "the devil's counterfiet."[6]

The second great weakness of the early fundamentalist efforts was any authenticating voice from the scientific community. Rimmer claimed scientific credentials but had no degree. Price digested enormous amounts of material but had no credentials from any scientific institution of higher learning. Indeed, he seemed antieducation much of the time. Bryan was a politician, and Riley a preacher. All of this changed with Henry M. Morris.

Henry M. Morris has become the prime "mover and shaker" in the current creationist fight against evolution.—Morris's view of creationism bears much similarity to earlier statements by George McCready Price. Keystones in his arch are that the world is less than ten thousand years old; that all things were created in six literal twenty-four-hour days; and that the Flood caused the geological strata which are interpreted as evidence for the evolutionary process.

Others have joined Morris in his effort to halt the spread of evolutionary teaching. One early colleague was James C. Whitcomb, Jr., with whom Morris collaborated in publishing *The Genesis Flood.* Morris was then chairing the civil engineering department at Virginia Polytechnic Institute, and Whitcomb was a teacher in Old Testament studies at Grace Theological Seminary in Indiana. In 1963 the Creation Research Society was formed. A network of correspondence with other creationists began. At the end of its first decade, the society claimed 450 regular members who met the scientific qualifications, that is, persons with graduate degrees in scientific disciplines. Morris's current research center is called the Institute for Creation Research. In 1981 a graduate program was begun offering graduate degrees in various creation-oriented sciences.[7]

Those who think evolutionist theory to be an impregnable rock would do well to read through a series of books produced by Baker Book House, each entitled *A Symposium on Creation.*

Evolution as a Divine Process

Some theologians and philosophers embrace evolution as the process whereby God created and continues to create.—An early example of this was Henri Bergson (1859-1941), a Frenchman who received the 1927 Nobel literature prize. His book, *Creative Evolution* (1907), made an immense impression on a young Frenchman, Pierre Teilhard de Chardin, who was pursuing graduate studies both in theology as a Jesuit priest and in geology.

Teilhard de Chardin had a special interest in palaeontology, which is the study of past geological periods based upon the study of fossils. He came to believe that evolution was the process whereby God created new possibilities within the universe, including man. This might be described as a kind of divine "push" or "pull" behind the scheme of things. His wide scientific knowledge, plus his commitment as a priest drove him to try to unify the natural and the spiritual. Evolution, he believed, was still continuing. As a dedicated Christian priest, Teilhard saw all things being drawn toward Christ in a kind of Christ consciousness and social consciousness. In the modern world, Teilhard visioned God as working more in the areas of cultural and social change than in genetic or biological change. His most famous book is *The Phenomenon of Man.*

Christian mysticism often embraces evolution.—One spinoff from the work by Teilhard de Chardin has been the appropriation of the concept of evolution by Christian mystics, especially Quakers. One Quaker defines mysticism "as a sense of being known and loved unconditionally, without reservations or restrictions, for oneself alone. There follows the paradox of feeling that one was never so much oneself or, at the same time, so . . . in a sense of identification with the divine."[8] Some Quaker mystics seem more prone toward a Christ-centered mysticism than others. Many modern Quaker mystics see evolution and depth psychology as confirmation of the mystical way. For example, John R. Yungblut states: "As I see it, emphasis on the mystical is supported by the fresh revelation that has flowed from the discovery of the fact of evolution and the accumulating insights emerging from depth psychology in this last century."[9] The key names in this emphasis are Teilhard de Chardin in evolution and Carl Jung in his studies of the human psyche. The new emphasis upon the spiritual and mystical side of human personality is to some Quakers a confirmation that a new evolutionary push is taking place in the world today. "The emerging, evolving human consciousness can be identified, I believe, as the mystical or contemplative faculty. One begins to see that the evolving spirituality of the earth itself can be understood as taking the shape of a new mysticism."[10]

From the previous survey it should be obvious that responses to evolution by Christians have been diverse. Between the two extremes mentioned are all shades of the spectrum of belief. Many are simply confused. One thing that might be helpful would be a new way of looking at the issue.

The Creative Process

As is obvious from studying creation, God was both artist and engineer/designer in putting His universe together. Since our concepts about evolution, either for or against, have come from science, we might be helped by taking a look from another vantage point. One way to do so is to study creativity. Since we are made in the image of God, human creativity might give us some hints about divine creativity.

The Right Side of the Brain

Studies in recent years have proposed that our minds work from both sides of the brain, the two sides fulfilling different functions.[11] The left side of the brain is the verbal side. It analyzes, plans, looks after details, reasons logically, is aware of time, and so forth. It manages our lives and thinks in a logical fashion from *since* to *therefore*. In short, the left side of our brain is the scientist, philosopher, engineer, and manager of our lives. The right side of our brain is the creative, dreaming, spontaneous, emotional, part of us. Time is often irrelevant when one is working out of the right side of the brain. Artists and musicians who lose all track of time are examples of this phenomenon.

One side or the other is usually dominant in an individual. Artists use in a dominant way the right side of the brain. Scientists and lawyers use in a dominant way the left side of the brain. This is a partial explanation for the scholar who wouldn't recognize an emotion if it met him on Main Street and for an artist who never keeps an appointment and can't balance the checkbook. If you will read the Gospels with this feature in the back of your mind, you will see that Jesus was a perfect blend of both. If you will look at the universe, you will see that creation is balanced with both.

Part of our problem in handling the evolution controversy is that the thinking has been mostly from the left side of the brain. The mind has another side. The side of the brain that is creative ought also to be speaking about creation. At least it ought to have a say. But the creative folk haven't written on creation or evolution. They are out being creative in their own niche. Consider the irony of it all. Those who are best at managing and classifying facts write the books on how creation happened. These books in turn provide the windows through which all of us look at creation and evolution. Thus our viewpoints are given to us by those who may know the least about creativity. We need some balance. Notice two small examples. More work needs to be done in linking creativity with creation.

Creativity Rejoices in Options

One thing that surfaces soon in any study of creativity is that the creative person searches for options. Creativity finds different ways of doing the same thing. It also uses traditional methods to produce new results. In addition, creativity is always exploring new dimensions, new avenues of expression. All of this is determined by the mind and skill of the creative person. An illustration will help.

My wife is a potter. The other day I asked her, "How many ways could a potter make a simple clay bowl?" She thought for a moment and then began listing them as she thought of them. "You could throw it on the wheel, of course. Or you could build it by hand by using coils of clay. That is the way the American Indians did and do. Or you could build it by hand, using clay slabs. Or you could form it inside a basket like they did in primitive times. Or you could form it around a rock which provided the desired shape. Or you could do a simple pinch-pot. Or you could use a slip [liquid clay] in a plaster mold." She had listed seven ways to bring a simple clay bowl into being. "How would you know which one to use?" I asked. "The kind of clay you were using would have something to do with it," she said. "Also the amount of skill the potter has would be a factor." I went one step further. "Would you be able to tell which process was used after it was finished?" I continued. She nodded. "A good potter usually could. However, Indians build with coils so well that they often look like they've been thrown on a wheel."

In the evolutionary debate, the scientists say they have discovered *the* process whereby living organisms have acquired the characteristics which distinguish them. Isn't that a bit limiting? One truth about creativity is that usually several ways or processes to accomplish the same thing exist. If a potter has seven options on how to create a simple clay pot, how many more processes would God have at His disposal to create the world and the organisms within it? Ten? A hundred? Hundreds? Thousands? To assume that God would do everything one way is against everything we know about creativity. To assume that we have discovered all, or even a fraction of those processes, is arrogance. On the other hand, to declare that God could *not* have created some segment of His creation in a certain way is to limit His sovereign options as Creator.

Creativity and Delegation

One of the most creative sides of management is delegation. We have seen how God delegated to Adam certain responsibilities. Delegation is not abdication. Nor is it supervision. The best delegators use two principles. They are constantly reviewing, yet they create enough space to allow the process of delegation to work. We see this in the account of Adam in the garden. God delegated to Adam the care of creation, the naming of the animals and their care. On the other hand, He did not walk off and leave creation. His presence was there. The universe was sustained by His Word. He came to Adam and Eve in their trouble.

The theological words for these two principles of delegation are transcendence and immanence. Transcendence means above and apart from. Immanence means indwelling, a part of. The paradox of God's relationship with His world is that He is both above and apart from, yet He is present, He dwells within. On a human level, all good delegation has both of these dimensions. Workers know that the boss is apart from them, above them. Yet they can sometimes sense his presence even when he is not visible. The best bosses create enough freedom for others to do their work, yet are always aware of what is going on. Sometimes the boss moves in to do something new or adjust something old.

Sometimes delegation is to others, sometimes to machines. Machines like computers process things for us. We are tending more and more in that direction on a human level. We are still the ones who must make decisions. We are still in control. We are the ones who build in the process (programming), and we oversee its operation and outcome. If we are made in God's image, is it not likely God would exercise this same tendency on a cosmic scale? Instead of machines, He would have processes at His disposal that we cannot even imagine. Creation out of nothing is not something we can comprehend. But delegation to an impersonal process is something we can understand.

Sometimes delegation stops in the middle of a process. At that point, the master's hand is needed. For instance, in major hospitals where surgeons do the most intricate kinds of surgery, others often will "open" and "close." But when it comes time for the most important part of the procedure, the master surgeon does the work. If we tend in this direction, made in His image, why not God? This coincides with the biblical picture of God appearing on the scene, forming Adam and breathing into him the breath of divine life. When it is time for the Master's touch, the Master's skill, the Master's breath, He is there.

The current debate on evolution either sees God involved in nothing—only the process is at work. Or it sees God personally doing everything—no processes or delegation involved. Why not both? We do both. Yet this does not detract from the fact we are still the decision makers, the dreamers, the leaders, the makers, the designers. Delegation, whether to man or machine, simply helps us accomplish our purposes.

At the least, creativity provides another way of looking at the whole issue of creation and evolution. In the meantime, there are some questions that keep coming up from generation to generation, caused by the evolution controversy.

Some Specific Questions

The Bible doesn't deal with everything we ask about. Once theologians were debating how many angels could stand on the point of a needle. Would you think that worthy of scriptural space? Many of our questions may look that silly someday. The following questions would seem worthy if for no other reason than that they keep coming up. They are not answered specifically in the Bible. Every believer is called to interpret and free to interpret. The answers to each are only suggestive.

How Old Is the Universe?

Science uses billions in speaking of the age of the universe. Creationism speaks in terms of ten thousand years. The Bible doesn't say how old the universe is. In the first account of creation, it does say creation happened in six days. Does it refer to a literal twenty-four-hour day? Could it mean era or period of time? Either interpretation is legitimate. The Hebrew word is used both ways.

It is interesting to notice that as far back as Augustine, *day* was taken to mean a long period of time. At the turn of this century, R. A. Torrey used this to defend the Scripture against attack by those seeking to discredit the Genesis account. His interpretation of *day* bears repeating.

> Anyone at all familiar with the Bible knows that the use of the word "day" is not limited to periods of twenty-four hours. It is frequently used of a period of time of undefined length (e.g. see Joel 3:18; Zech. 2:10, 11; Zech. 13:1, 2:14, 9). There is no necessity whatever of interpreting the days of Gen. 1 as solar days of twenty-four hours. They may be vast periods of undefined length. "But," some one may say, "this is twisting the Scriptures to make them fit the conclusions of modern science." The one who says so simply displays his ignorance of the history of Biblical interpretation. St. Augustine, as far back as the fourth century, centuries before modern geology and its conclusions were dreamed of, interpreted the days of Gen. 1 as periods of time, just as the word means in many places elsewhere in the Bible.[12]

Geology stretches the age of the world out because it is thought the best explanation for the facts. For instance, the hydrocarbons from which petroleum products come are often in desert places which were once ocean bottoms. Oil and natural gas were derived originally from organic remains, both plants and animals.[13] The hydrocarbons develop when the organic material is buried beneath layers of earth and rock. With increasing burial the temperature and pressure increases. When a certain depth is reached, changes begin to take place in the organic material. The original molecules are broken down into new molecules which begin to form hydrocarbon liquid and gas within the rock.[14] Obviously, an immense amount of time is required for this to happen. First, enough time must have elapsed in our world for oceans to become deserts. Then the breakdown of the molecules into hyrocarbons must have time to happen.

If the universe is as young as creationists say it is, two assumptions have to be made. First, that the upheaval noticed in geological strata occured during a universal flood. Second, that God created the world from the beginning with the hydrocarbons and other phenomenon already within the crust of the earth. The question is not whether He could have. The question is, why would He?

What About the Cave Men?

The Bible doesn't deal with what are called in some schoolbooks cave men, or prehistoric man. What the Bible does deal with is the creation of man as a unique act of the Creator, made in God's image, and responsible before God who is his Creator. In our minds, we usually place this event alongside the beginning of civilization. Maybe so, maybe not. It is not man's civilized veneer which links man to God. It is his inner childlike self. We usually call this the "heart." Jesus said, "Unless you turn and become like children, you will never enter the kingdom of heaven" (Matt. 18:3). The important moment was that instant when God breathed into Adam His own breath. From then on a spiritual being existed.

Was There Only One Adam?

If evolution is thought to be the process by which man came into being, it is natural to think of this happening the world over at approximately the same time. Thus, the theory is, there would have been several Adams, so to speak. Such reflection sets aside the uniqueness of Adam as a creative work of God. It is not nature which creates Adam's uniqueness, but the special act of the Creator. If Adam is unique by God's creative will, he is a first. God doesn't create clones.

The Real Issue

The real issue, however, is not *how* God created His universe. The critical issue for Christian belief is in another arena. It is the blurring of the distinction between the Creator and the process. To many, the process has become creator. Along with chance, evolution has become the designer behind all things. The Creator has been even further removed from His creation. To that issue we must now give our best attention.

Notes

1. Charles Darwin, *The Descent of Man, and Selection in Relation to Sex* (London: John Murray, 1877), p. vi.
2. Irving Stone, *The Origin* (New York: A Plume Book), p. 384.
3. *World Book Encyclopedia,* Vol. 6 (Chicago: Field Enterprises Educational Corporation, 1968), pp. 332,3.
4. Quoted by Ronald L. Numbers, "Creationism in 20th-Century America," *Science,* Vol. 218, Nov. 5, 1982, p. 540.
5. Ibid.
6. Ibid., p. 542.
7. Ibid.

8. John R. Yungblut, "Variations on the Quaker Message: The Mystical Emphasis," *Friends Journal,* Vol. 30, No. 18, December 1, 1984, p. 4.

9. Ibid.

10. Ibid.

11. Sally P. Springer and Georg Deutsch, *Left Brain, Right Brain* (San Francisco: W.H. Freeman and Company, 1981), p. 46.

12. R.A. Torrey, *Hard Problems of Scripture* (Chicago: Rams Horn Company, 1906), p. 1.

13. L. Don Leet, Sheldon Judson, and Marvin E. Kauffman, *Physical Geology* (New Jersey: Prentice Hall, Inc., 1978), p. 352.

14. Ibid., p. 354.

8

Evolution as Substitute Creator

Let us begin this chapter by looking at two pictures by which to live. For ultimately that is what we wind up doing, living by the great images and events in which we believe and to which we are committed.

Two Pictures

The first is given to us by the apostle John at the beginning of the Gospel which bears his name. The Word, he said, which from the beginning spoke the worlds into being, is none other than the One who confronts us in Jesus Christ our Lord. John further declared that this Word which was from the beginning and created all things is the same Word of life and love which was spoken through the birth, life, death, and resurrection of our Lord. This creative Word is not unrelated to His creation. Instead He is dedicated to the restoration of creation through grace and truth (John 1:1-18). The picture is that of the Creator humbling Himself to assume the life of a human being. He lowered Himself that we might rise to new heights of life and love. He became like us so that, in some small way at least, we could become like Him. This is the picture of the new creation God is about. It is potential within every person.

Now let me give you another picture. It is provided by a most distinguished scientist, Edward Teller, in his book *Energy from Heaven and Earth.*[1] The book has been of great assistance in helping me understand energy, its origin and usage, and the energy problems we face. However, as with many books, I don't agree with everything in it. Teller is a renowned physicist and worked extensively on nuclear developments both before and after World War II. In showing the sources for fossil fuels—coal, oil, natural gas—he shows how plant life came to exist on earth. In discussing its origins, he begins by discussing the origins of life on earth.

> No one knows how life originated on earth (or rather, in the sea). Was it an extremely improbable chance? Did the germ of life arrive from outside of earth? (This of course would not answer the basic question about the *origin* of life. It means only that we pass the buck.) In fact we can't even define life, much less state how it started. Following an ancient tradition one may say the origin of life was miraculous.

Teller then goes on to explain how life started in the oceans. The nutrients life needed, he suggests, came from the skies and established a kind of soup in which life could flourish. How was the extinction of life averted?

> Extinction was averted by a splendid discovery, and this discovery is not fancy but fact.
>
> Of course, this discovery was not made by a conscious effort. It was rather, made in the peculiar fashion in which most great and remarkable discoveries in the living world arise; by lots of trials and almost as many errors. The infinitesimal residue of successes is known as *evolution.* The name of the discovery was *chlorophyll.*
>
> Chlorophyll is an extremely complex chemical substance designed to utilize sunlight. . . . No one has succeeded in duplicating that action in a test tube. So far, only chlorophyll within living plants is able to utilize sunlight in this peculiar and tricky manner. . . . It is probable that the discovery of chlorophyll did not occur in one step. Chlorophyll may have been the final result of a lengthy evolution, but we can describe what it accomplished once it got into action.

Dr. Teller is not on trial here. My purpose is to deal with the picture that he draws for us.

Two pictures have been presented. Both are about life. Both relate to the world we live in. The first pictures of One who created all things as the Author of life. This One, said John, became flesh and dwelt among us that we might be restored to the source of all life, God the Creator. The second picture is about the origins of life and about how things have come down to us. According to this picture, no rational processes were involved in the origin of life. The world got here by "many trials and almost as many errors." The first picture is of the God who loves to create and who creates love. The second is of a world fashioned by impersonal forces and designed by unconscious choices of chance. Persons usually live by and believe in one of these two pictures. We will concentrate on the second picture, that of Evolution in this chapter. The picture of the new creation follows in the chapter entitled, "The Creator as Redeemer." Evolution will be given a capital *E* in this chapter to signify the difference between evolution as a process and Evolution as a substitute creator.

Evolution as Designer

Chlorophyll, it turns out, is an extremely complex chemical substance. It is so complex, in fact, that man has not been able to duplicate it. At this point in time, all man can do is study its effectiveness and describe what it accomplishes. However, all of this came about by trial and error, according to Dr. Teller. "The discovery was not made by a conscious effort."

Creation Without Conscious Effort

What this implies is that a discovery not made by conscious effort turns out to be superior to any yet made by man. In other words, the impersonal force called Evolution, which makes selection by trial and error, has discovered (created?) something which baffles the best minds. How can this be? Man's mind has been involved in all of the breakthroughs of science. Take the inquisitive mind of man away from the laboratory and you have nothing but bare walls and equipment. Of course, even the bare walls and the equipment are products of the mind of man. It is mind that makes experimentation work. Indeed, we would not even know about the existence of chlorophyll if it were not for creative, scientific minds doing research.

If chlorophyll is a discovery superior to any man has been able to make, does this not imply a superior Mind creating or inventing it? Can you think of any instance in scientific discovery which has excluded the mind of the scientists? Then how can that which the scientific mind studies be the product of nonconscious choices? If there is no such thing as nonconscious investigation, can there be such a thing as nonconscious creation?

Trial and Error

Scientific discoveries have been made by trial and error. Some times they have been literally "bumped into." This is the image that we get from evolutionary change. But let us look behind the whole possibility of trial and error. For trial and error to exist, possibilities must exist. But possibilities must be created. And the only way we know of that possibilities can be created is through the use of the mind.

A scientist in research and development deals constantly with possibilities. Human relations counselors constantly try to get their clients to think of new possibilities. Suicide often comes when the mind ceases to think of new possibilities. Sales people and motivational people speak of possibility thinking. The point is that we *think* of possibilities. Take the mind away and we no longer think, and therefore we no longer think of possibilities.

Many of us have watched beloved relatives come to their later years without full possession of their minds. Age or disease has taken its toll. Possibilities easily met in former days are no longer attainable. In fact, one of the first casualities of a weakened mind is the inability to think of alternatives. Mind and possibility are linked. When the mind goes, so does possibility thinking.

We are dealing with a domino effect. To have trial and error, possibilities must exist. To have possibilities, a mind must be at work. One might say, "But there may be possibilities we haven't thought of." True. But if they are found, they will have been thought of. And that is just the point. It is impossible for us to think of trial and error without bringing the mind into play. To speak of a discovery not made by conscious effort is to speak about that of which we know nothing. Nor can any scientific experiment prove that such is possible. Those who believe such do so as an unspoken creed from the point of view of their belief system, not out of scientific objectivity.

The belief that the mind of the Creator is behind all things is at least as coherent as the other. If the Creator is about what we believe He is about, chlorophyll is exactly what we should expect. That we should not, as yet, be able to duplicate it is no reflection upon us or the Creator. Nor will it change anything if we eventually discover how He did it. What is difficult to comprehend is how chlorophyll could have been invented without a Mind behind it.

Irrational Creation?

The next question with which we must deal is whether reason is involved at all in creation. If evolutionary choices are not conscious choices, they are irrational choices. For what the mind does, among other things, is reason. Without reason, part of which is memory, we could do virtually nothing.

When, in our modern world, changes are made, we inevitably alter the natural state of things. We do this rationally. We build bridges, plan highways, fly airplanes, and split atoms. In each instance, we alter nature to some extent. In every instance, reason is involved. Even when we decide to set aside a national park so that nature will be unchanged, we *choose* to set it aside. We make rules, rationally, to preserve it that way. C. S. Lewis called this the "colonisation of Nature by Reason." "Every object you see before you at this moment —the walls, ceiling, and furniture, the book, your own washed hands and cut fingernails, bears witness to the colonisation of Nature by Reason: for none of this matter would have been in these states if Nature had had her way."[2]

Scientific discovery always involves the colonization of nature by reason and often the alteration of nature by reason. Think of how many experiments on rats are done each year in the name of science. Nature is altered. Every time an atom is split, nature is altered. Every instance of laser beam technology involves an alteration of and colonization of nature. None of this colonization or alteration is done apart from human reason. Nature, left untended, does not reason or discover. Reason, acting upon nature, colonizing and altering, discovers. Discovery without reason is a reality of which we cannot conceive. This is what Evolution without conscious choice implies.

The Networking of Reason

One person's reason develops a kind of network with the reason of other persons, and a kind of building-block effect results. Thus each generation has the opportunity to learn from the previous generations. Science has advanced by leaps and bounds because new generations have been able to connect with the reasoned work done by previous scientists.

In nature, man alone seems to be capable of this networking effect, this building-block possibility reaching from one generation to the next. The swallows may return to Capistrano each year but they are not apt to invent an airplane to take them there and pass the aerodynamic plans from one generation to the next. When Evolution is spoken of as a substitute creator, a networking effect is implied. It is as if nature conspires to build upon that which has been done to produce the next new step.

Notice Dr. Teller's speaking of chlorophyll as probably being the end of a process, the final result of several steps of evolution actively at work. A networking is suggested in his discussion. But network building is not something nature can be observed to do. Man does this because he links his reason with other reasoning persons. Behind this networking are minds. If there is a networking principle operative in nature, a Mind must be at work in there somewhere.

Incidentally, Christian experience reveals a networking between the believer and God's mind. If man is made in the image of God, mind is part of that image. Networking with God's mind and Spirit is just what we would expect. Nature cannot be observed to provide a network of building blocks for the next generation.

Reason as a Product of Evolution

Some would explain mind and reason as products of Evolution itself. Thus the mind of man is a kind of pinnacle to which the pyramid of evolutionary choices has pointed all along. This seems logical enough. The difficulty with this position is that, if this is true, all creation before man would be creatively inferior. But this is not what we find. Some facets of creation are incredibly complex. They bear the reflection of an inventiveness that man can only approximate.

Chlorophyll is a good example. It came before man, and yet reflects an inventive intelligence superior to man. If man cannot invent it, how can the mind of man be the pinnacle of Evolution? If chlorophyll is at the lower end of the evolutionary ladder and the mind of man at the top, inventing chlorophyll ought to be a snap. Since the mind of man has yet to catch up to the secret behind chlorophyll, does this not suggest that a Mind greater than man's was about this business of creation from the beginning?

Evolution as the reason behind reason is caught in a massive contradiction. If Evolution created the human mind by chance, then reason is not involved in the creation of the human mind. But this means believing in creativity without mind and without reason. On the other hand, if the human mind was created reasonably, that is with reason, something more than chance is behind it.

Evolution as a Belief System

In summary, Evolution, with a capital *E,* has become the stackpole around which a new belief system has arisen. Key doctrines in this secular creedalism (remember, secular is defined in this book as the organization of life without God), are as follows: 1. Nature, or the universe, is the "Whole Show"; 2. All things came into being by chance; 3. Evolution caused things to get like they are by trial and error. This is the unspoken secular trinity: nature, chance, and Evolution.

Evolution as Designer

We have seen that the concept of evolution has evolved from process to cause. Evolution is thus seen as the power behind the design of the universe and man. We have already seen how difficult it is to conceive of Evolution as the cause behind all things, when its basic operational principle is trial and error, apart from mind and reason. Perhaps the easiest way to focus on this difficulty is to center on the concept of Evolution as designer or inventor.

If Evolution is the cause of all things, it has uncanny abilities to design. It is amazingly adept as a scientist, engineer, ecologist, and inventor. To replace the Creator, who by His nature is a designer, with Evolution, whose basic method of operation is trial and error, is to make a really stout substitution. A few illustrations will help to show, by way of contrast, what this substitution means.

What About the Design of the Human Heart?

The human body is an incredible organism. Almost any part would be worthy of humble admiration. Our question here is the origin of its invention, if I may use the word *invention* in this instance. To narrow the subject, simply consider the invention and design of the human heart.

During the year that I have been writing this book, another artificial heart transplant has been attempted. It has garnered the headlines. Reports on the patient's welfare have been printed daily throughout the nation. For all of this let us give thanks. The Savior said, "Greater things than I do, will you do." Perhaps this is an example of it. However, as I understand the artificial heart, it is made operative by a "driver" which is a pump that works outside the human body and which provides the power to circulate the blood through the artificial heart.

Now the marvelous people who put together that artificial heart and its accompanying pump are truly amazing. With their experimentation, their creative minds, their imaginative spirits, they are on the brink of putting together what we call a miracle of medical science. Can you image that artificial heart being designed, the pump being designed and manufactured, the patient being cared for, the surgeons doing their work, without personal minds behind it all? Consider all of the many people involved in an operation such as this and all of the minds given to the development of an artificial heart. To imagine any of this coming about without the creativity and imagination of the mind is impossible. Yet that is what Evolution is supposed to have done in coming up with the heart pumping in your breast right now.

Take a look at the real thing. The heart which we carry around inside of us not only has the valves but the pump itself. What an amazing invention! Suppose we gathered together all of the wise inventors, engineers, and medical researchers and said to them, "Invent the human heart." What would they need to consider? They would need a compact, automatic pump which would operate at only a fraction of a horsepower. It would need to be light enough to be carried around inside the chest cavity leaving room for all of the other bodily functions to work. This would mean about ten ounces in a man and about eight ounces in a woman. In short, it would need to be about the size of a human fist.

The heart pump being invented would need to do an incredible amount of work over an extended period of time. The work done by this pump each minute would need to be equivalent to lifting seventy pounds one foot off of the ground. Furthermore, this pump would have to be able to replenish itself with new cells regularly and periodically so that it could sustain its work over a lifetime. For the most part, this pump would need to idle smoothly beating about forty million strokes a year, yet it must be sensitive to any increase or decrease in the fluid being pumped, responding immediately by acceleration or deceleration without having to be prompted by rational processes. It must be strong enough to do its work, yet soft enough so that its valve closure must not damage millions of cells which form almost half of the volume of fluid that it is pumping.

Everybody knows that moving machinery needs smooth lubricated surfaces. This would mean that the pump which is being invented would need to be constantly lubricated. But since the human body has no place to replace lubrication such as an oil spout or a grease fitting, the lubrication would have to be supplied from internal body sources, which are constantly replenished. Also the heart pump would have to be designed so that it could move, beat, and do its work while not pulling and tugging at other body organs nearby. Incidentally, the way in which the Creator solved this problem was by creating the pericardium, a kind of wet slippery bag which encases the heart. Pericardium means literally, "the thing around the heart." The bag allows the necessary freedom of movement the heart has to have and the protection other parts of the chest cavity have to have, all of the time providing a smooth, lubricated surface inside which the heart can do its work.

The preceding paragraphs would make up but a small section of any specification list for inventing the human heart. That group of inventors, engineers, and medical research scientists would have their work cut out for them. But just suppose that they would be able to invent the miracle we call the human heart. Not an artificial heart with a pump outside, understand, but a real bona fide replacement. The whole world would beat a path to their doorstep. The media would be absolutely fascinated and enchanted. Specials on television would center not only on the result of their work but also on them. Their lives would be spotlighted, their backgrounds researched, their accomplishments cataloged.

One thing would not happen. There would be no emphasis upon the heart that was invented in the first place. Yet that heart, taken for granted, keeps each of us going every day. It demands nothing from our concentration. It often works under the liabilities of our life-styles. And many of us are living seventy, eighty, and even a hundred years.

Now what we are being asked to accept is that the amazing invention of the human body, including the human heart, came about through the mindless process, the hit-and-miss ingenuity of trial and error we call Evolution. Anyone who believes that the human body was invented without a mind, designer, engineer, scientist, and physician behind it is a "true believer" in the secular doctrines of life. There is certainly no evidence that such a marvelous invention could come into being in this way.

What About Ecology?

If Evolution, as the impersonal force behind creation, can ever claim supremacy, it should be in its own backyard, that of nature. Ecology ought to be its major. With that in mind, let's take a look at the delight of every gardener, and the bane of every neighbor, the compost pile.

What got me to thinking about this was a compost pile that was the gift of my predecessor in the home I now enjoy. It had accumulated for many years. That marvelous humus has now been distributed throughout the yard and enriched the soil, loosening the basic clay structure of our garden area. How did it come to pass that those leaves, twigs, scraps from the table, and other material placed there were made worthy of being recycled in my garden?

It all begins by designing a world which continually reproduces and replenishes itself. Reproduction is crucial. If forests, grasses, flowers, birds, fish, and bees did not constantly reproduce, in a short time the entire world would be barren. "Only God can make a tree," the poem said which we were taught in school. Even more remarkable, however, is a tree that makes another tree. Reproduction is something, with all of our heady scientific advance, we've not even begun to approximate. Perhaps its just as well. Plastic cups and tin cans need no proliferation, not to speak of rusty cars and broken bottles.

In addition to reproduction, trees, grasses, and the food we eat all need to be made of materials that will deteriorate and, in doing so, supply nourishment for microscopic guests who eat the bounty thus produced. The microscopic guests, in turn, produce humus which is essential for good rich soil. The design of our world is incredibly efficient and effective.

The compost of the gardener is a marvel of ecological engineering. Cecil E. Johnson, professor of natural history, Riverside City College, California, described it like this.[3] It is like a miniature universe inhabited by myriad creatures, smaller than beasts of the forests, but just as wild. Astronomical numbers of microbial short-order cooks, called aerobic (oxygen-consuming) bacteria, shoot the temperature up to 131 degrees Fahrenheit so that the waste is broken down into soft, mushy, easily rotted wastes. The compost pile is also populated by millions of nematodes, tiny cylindrical microscopic worms, which feast on the decaying material. One nematode authority painstakingly counted approximately 90,000 in one rotting apple! Other residents also take up large portions of real estate in that seemingly worthless heap. As the bacteria go to work decomposing the material, insects and worms eat the decaying vegetation and excrete organic compounds. Tunneling as they go, they aerate the compost and therefore increase the area where microbes can feed. It is an incredible system of complex biochemistry. When the process is completed, compost is made which, when mixed with soil, allows air and water to penetrate more easily and water retention increases, limiting nutrient runoff and soil erosion. It is all a marvelous ecological system that operates completely independent of any human agent, although steps can be taken to hurry the process along.

Let's go back to that compost heap left by my predecessor. As often happens, some things get mixed in that are not part of nature's produce. There was a paper cup, a cellophane candy wrapper, a cigarette wrapper, a piece of a broken flower pot, and a piece of a glass bottle. None of these deteriorated. And all of them were made by man. None were recycled naturally. No usefulness is observable from their continued existence. Whoever or whatever designed the ecological program of nature was far more advanced in ecological planning, design, and engineering than anything we can approximate. Which means that Whoever or whatever designed the ecological system of our world was a lot smarter than we are. We can't even figure out what to do with our nuclear wastes!

So we are back at a crucial choice again. Either the silent, incredibly balanced, efficient, yet people-friendly ecological program was put together by a mindless force, or it was put together by a personal designer we call the Creator. We are back at a basic: Trial and error don't create and don't design. They choose from existing realities. Who created the realities?

Belief in Evolution as maker or designer is not a position provable by science. It is a part of a secular creed. Others call the Christian faith a creed. It is much more than that as every believer knows. But if that is all it is, at least it respects the place of mind and reason in Creation. To use Dorothy Sayre's phrase, we believe the universe is the result of the mind of the Maker. By experience, we know that Creator personally. He has "networked" His Spirit and mind into our lives, so that even now we reasonate with the touch of His very being. Is the worship of Evolution much better, after all, than the worship of a lifeless, mindless idol?

Notes

1. Edward Teller, *Energy from Heaven and Earth* (San Francisco: W. H. Freeman and Company, 1979), pp. 39-40.
2. C.S. Lewis, *Miracles* (New York: Macmillan, 1963), p. 26.
3. Cecil E. Johnson, "The Wild World of Compost," *National Geographic*, Vol. 158, No. 2, August 1980, pp. 273-284.

9

The Creator as Redeemer

A story has come from the days when horseless carriages were replacing horsedrawn carriages. A gentleman had taken his new machine out for a drive, only to have it break down. Knowing little about machines and almost nothing about automobiles, he raised the hood. Presently a kindly gentleman came by in his own horseless carriage and stopped to assist. He looked things over, went back to his own car for a toolbox, and went to work. In a while, he asked the owner of the car to turn the crank. The car started immediately. The man in distress thanked his visitor profusely and then asked, "Where did you learn how to fix these new machines?" The man with the tools replied, "I ought to know how to fix them. I made them. My name is Henry Ford."

In the greatest life ever lived, God, who made all things, came to earth to provide His creation the possibility of repair. The word we often use for this effort of God in behalf of His world is *redemption. Redeem* is a word wrung out of ancient life. It means to buy back something which formerly belonged to the purchaser but had passed out of his possession. When it is used as an expression of God's action, it implies something God does to buy back the world which once was His by creation. The way in which He does this is through His sacrificial love expressed fully in Jesus Christ the Lord. *Redemption* is a word which declares that God is not a quitter. He has not nor will He give up on His world. He will, in fact, do everything possible to get it back on track without violating the freedom of man to decide and the freedom of man to relate.

The Old and the New

Faith preserves its insights like beavers build dams. Each new breakthrough builds upon that which was and preserves that which is new. Jesus described one who was adequately prepared for the kingdom of Heaven to be "like a householder who brings out of his treasure what is new and what is old" (Matt. 13:52). So it is with creation. The New Testament claims the truth of the Old Testament doctrine of creation. The new treasure is that which has been made possible through Jesus Christ the Lord. "Therefore, if any one is in Christ, he is a new creation, the old has passed away, behold the new has come" (2 Cor. 5:17).

The new creation is not some recent development which God devised because things were not going well. Rather, the same One who brings the new creation is the One who initiated the old. "Yet for us there is one God, the Father, from whom are all things and for whom we exist, and One Lord, Jesus Christ, through whom all things and through whom we exist" (1 Cor. 8:6). The apostle Paul, who wrote these words, knew that for salvation to be effective, as well as for everyone, creation and redemption must center in one person. The excited declaration of the New Testament is that this centering has happened in Jesus Christ the Lord.

The reason the New Testament is so optimistic, in spite of the weaknesses of man, is that the will of God to redeem is equal to the will of God to create. This is by no means an obvious and natural idea. It dawned upon a dulled world like a needed thrust of light. The Creator and the Redeemer are One! When we encounter One, we meet the Other. He alone has the power to create the possibilities of creation and salvation. He alone has the knowledge to reveal what is wrong and what can be put right. He alone has the eternal presence to sustain both the universe and the spiritual life. Nowhere is it more beautifully presented than in the three great hymns which portray the Creator as Redeemer.

Redemption Through the Incarnation
John 1:1-14

The first great hymn to the Creator as Redeemer that I want to mention is found at the beginning of John's Gospel. He began with praise to the Word who created all things in the beginning.

> In the beginning was the Word, and the Word was with God and the Word was God. He was in the beginning with God; all things were made through him, and without him was not anything made that was

made. In him was life, and the life was the light of men. The light shines in the darkness, and the darkness has not overcome it (John 1:1-5).

John began where the Scripture begins, at that eternal dawn when God spoke the cosmos into being through His Word. As we saw earlier in the Genesis 1 hymn of creation, God did not fashion the world, shape it, tool it, or craft it. He spoke it into being through His Word. The Hebrew word for *create* in that first Genesis hymn is *bara.* It is used sparingly in the Old Testament and reserved for those times when God is creating something new. In all the creative acts of God, the Word was the One responsible.

Dimensions of the Word

This Word was *eternal:* "In the beginning." It was not part of the created order which will eventually pass away. The Word was *relational:* "The Word was with God." Within the Godhead, or within the being of God Himself, there is a relational dimension. Note for instance Genesis 1:26, "Let *us* make man in our image, after our likeness" (author's italics). The Word was *divine:* "The Word was God." Thus, John's hymn not only praises the Word but also sees that the Word alone has the power necessary to heal man, put him back on the right track, and create in him new possibilities. The help that man needs must be *eternal,* greater than time and space. The power must be *personal,* able to relate to and communicate with man. The help must be from the Creator, *divine,* for only the Creator truly understands the creature.

Life and Light

In addition, this Word which is eternal, relational, and divine is life and light. "In Him was life, and the life was the light of men." Notice that the order is reversed in eternity. Life precedes light. On earth, light precedes life. In the eternities only God understands, light is but a dimension of God's life, although light is, and remains one of the most powerful symbols pointing to that life.

Life then is the earliest mentioned characteristic of the Word. Life is the joyous nature of the Word that creates. John followed this theme throughout the gospel. For example, Jesus says: "I am come that they might have life, and that they might have it more abundantly" (John 10:10*b,* KJV). After Lazarus died, Jesus said to Martha, "I am the resurrection and the life" (John 11:25). Martha was assured by the Word whose very nature is that of life. Jesus spoke, and Lazarus was raised from death to life. In the closing words of the twentieth chapter, John summarized the work of Christ with this triumph: "These [words] are written that you may believe that Jesus is the Christ, the Son of God, and that believing you may have life in his name" (v. 31).

The Word is still in the eternal business of creating life. But the Word which creates life could have become the best-kept secret in the universe if kept in heaven. The Word needed a human dimension—seeable, knowable, understandable. This is where Christ comes in.

Grace and Truth

The hymn peaks in the declaration that the Word which was eternal, relational, and divine had become flesh. "And the Word became flesh and dwelt among us, full of grace and truth; we have beheld his glory, glory as of the only Son from the Father" (John 1:14). The Word which spoke the cosmos into being and placed the worlds into His eternal frame has entered that world. The world has felt the redeeming presence of the Creator. The presence does not thunder from Mount Olympus or Mount Sinai with a new law but comes instead with heaven's word of grace. "For the law was given through Moses; grace and truth came through Jesus Christ" (v. 17). The world is to be redeemed not by additional boundaries but by the boundless grace of God as revealed in Christ the living Word. *Grace* means God's loving favor given to us not on the basis of our perfect performance but because we are persons He loves. Our lack of merit is matched by His unwillingness to put limits around His grace.

The Incarnation as the First Step in Redemption

The Creator, in order to become Redeemer and provide the grace that redeems, had to enter the human scene. A personal experience will assist in understanding why this is essential. Some years ago on a cold fall afternoon I went home to pick up a book. As I walked into the house, I heard a strange sound. Thump, thump, thump. I could not place it. Upon investigation, I discovered that the sound was caused by birds flying against a large plate glass window which looked out upon the yard. Some birds would strike the window and then fall lifeless to the ground. Upon a closer look, they turned out to be robins.

I turned the lights on, but perhaps because of the light outside, the inside light didn't create enough contrast to matter. The misdirection continued.

I decided to go out and try to frighten them away. Waving my arms and shouting, all I accomplished was to confuse them even more and increase their speed. Nothing I did was adequate to help them in their plight. Standing back and observing the whole scene, it suddenly occurred to me that the only way I could truly change the destructive pattern of those robins would be to become one. If I did, I could communicate in their language, using their images. I would then be able to not only explain the puzzle they could not put together but also explain the solution to it. They might not listen. But at least they would have been told the good news that there was an alternative to the way they were proceeding. Not until darkness came did the contrast between the light inside and the darkness outside turn them away.

The experience is a parable. It emphasizes the truth that if God was ever going to explain to us the solution to the puzzle of life He was going to have to become like we are. He was going to have to enter our world, experience our circumstances, and communicate with us, using our images. Since He did so He was not only able to explain the solution to the puzzle but also to provide an alternative solution.

It was not my option, of course, to become like a robin. For both the robin and I are creatures. But the Creator had an option which a creature does not have. It is the claim of the Christian faith that this is precisely what the Creator did in Jesus Christ. He entered the human scene and completely immersed Himself within it. The word for this is *incarnation.* Incarnation means "in the flesh." God entered the human situation in the flesh—"The Word became flesh and dwelt among us" (John 1:14).

Incarnation as Miracle

The thoughtful person asks, How can God enter the human scene? Can a novelist become a word and enter into his novel? Can a painter become a person painted and enter into his picture? The question is a good one, but typically human. First, we are asking questions within human categories. If God, who is life, chooses to enter that which is also life, it would demand a miracle but would not be contrary to His being. For as we have seen, life is God's very nature.

That the Creator would become incarnate is surprise enough. The surprise continues in the manner in which God became incarnate. Why not a Messiah full grown, riding out of the East, commanding all of the troops in the world to set wrong into right and straighten out the crookedness? Or, why not a full-grown King, entering the scene in Rome or Alexandria or Athens? But, of course, such an incarnation would make a mockery of the true human situation. The total immersion of God in His world included a birth, a manger, even a "No Vacancy" sign at the inn. Eventually it included suffering of the most bitter kind, rejection, and physical death. God fully entered His world that we might fully enter His kingdom. It is all sheer gift. It is His doing not ours.

How silently, how silently
The wondrous gift is giv'n!
So God imparts to human hearts
The blessings of his heav'n.

One of the reasons God takes the patient way of love is His stubborn refusal to violate the boundaries of freedom and relationships He set at creation. He will not manipulate us. Nor will He control us like puppets. In addition, He will not transgress our relational freedom. The kingdom, He said, is like the smallest of seeds, but it never quits growing (Mark 4:31). Headline grabbing is not its method.

By now it should be clear that redemption is not a stodgy, predictable event planned by an aged heavenly ruler. Eternal life obviously bears the imprint of joy, the bright hope of a smile, the dawn of surprise, and the incredible realization that God has alternatives we have never even dreamed of. The Word became flesh. The miracle is that it happened. The mystery is cradled in how He did it.

Redemption Pays the Price
Philippians 2:5-10

The second beautiful hymn that I want us to look at which lyrically speaks of the Creator turning Redeemer is in Philippians 2.

Who, being in very nature God,
   did not consider equality with God
   something to be grasped,
but made himself nothing,
   taking the very nature of a servant,

being made in human likeness.
And being found in appearance as a man,
he humbled himself and became obedient to death—
even death on a cross! (vv. 6-8, NIV).

Theologians have understood through the years that, in some way, redemption was going to have to pay a price. If the world turns on a moral hinge, the Creator designed it that way. Therefore, the evil in the world cannot be dealt with by pretending it isn't there. The injustice and sin that is in the world can't be answered with a divine wink. How then would God satisfy the requirement that justice be done for the cruelties, sins, and atrocities which are done in His world? The answer was that He would give Himself.

God's Design

As we try to see into God's design for getting us back on the right track again, one thing seems foremost. He was going to have to enter and live through, indeed suffer through, that which He spoke into being. If He withdrew from the whole scene, something within us would call out, "Unfair." Someone might object and point out that the troubles of the world are not God's fault. True. But man, his freedom, and the reality of evil exist because God allows them to exist. God taught Isaiah to understand this:

I form light and create darkness,
I make weal and create woe,
I am the Lord, who do all these things.
I made the earth,
and created man upon it;
it was my hands that stretched out the heavens,
and I commanded all their host. (Isa. 45:7,12).

God takes the awesome responsibility for what happens because He created in such a way that they could happen. If He withdrew, it could be said that God fled from the scene. Irresponsibility is not one of God's attributes.

Furthermore, God's withdrawal would put into motion all of the wrong responses. They might run something like this. "I had no choice in being born. It is not my doing that the world got created like it did. I didn't put it all together so there would be so much suffering and strife. I didn't choose to make a world where criminals roam the streets at night and nations wage war with each other. Come down here and live where I am living." This is the mood of Robert Frost's poem "A Question."

> A voice said, Look me in the stars
> And tell me truly, men of earth
> If all the soul-and-body scars
> Were not too much to pay for birth.[1]

Admittedly, there is some self-pity involved in those statements. But such feelings raise immense barriers to love and reunion with God. If God is interested in sons and daughters to love, He is going to have to take an approach other than simply blaming us for all the troubles in the world and withdrawing from the scene. Blame placing is not a divine attribute either.

A Dust Bowl Illustration

In James Michener's historical novel *Centennial,*[2] Dr. Creevey is a man who promoted the sale of range land in western Colorado at the beginning of this century. His idea was to put the land into crops, primarily wheat. Creevy insisted that dry-land farming would work and went abroad selling his gospel. Farmers from the East and the North took the challenge to move westward, homesteading on the land previously devoted to cattle and range.

What Creevey didn't count on were the dry years, or what section upon section of land, recently worked, would do when the wind absorbed the moisture from it. The tough years were 1934 and 1935. The area was called, "the dust bowl." Suddenly, rolling in from north and west, a universe of swirling dust, a blackness, would blot out the sun at noonday. In midday the sky was as dark as night and silt seeped through everything, every door, crack, and window. A weird gloom covered the earth. It was, in many ways, a nightmare from which many never recovered.

Creevey, it turned out, was partly right. A decade later, learning better to handle the soil, the vast plains area would provide wheat for the ever-increasing needs during World War II. But during the havoc of the thirties, farms were sold for taxes, some going for a dollar or fifty cents an acre and, in some instances, a used car so the one-time farmer could reach California. More important, the human devastation was terrifying. Minds and emotions gave way under the strain.

A sense of bitterness arose toward the man who got them into the situation in the first place. Creevey did come back to survey the desolation. Now an old man, he confessed he had made a mistake in teaching them how to farm. He had not seen what the great winds would do to loose soil in the years it didn't rain.

Those who survived the dust bowl have vivid memories of that time. I know. I was born in the dust bowl in 1934. The first time I finished Michener's chapter entitled "Drylands" I was shaking. I remembered the stories my mother used to tell. One was of losing sight of me when I was still crawling because she could not see her hand in front of her face. Crawling to where my cries were coming from, she found me, sitting under the ironing board, sobbing. We sat there for hours, handkerchiefs over our noses and eyes until the dust began to settle and my mother could see again. Michener's characters are, of course, fictional. The historical circumstances are not.

The story is a parable without an adequate ending. Something is missing. There is that within us which calls for those who create possibilities to come and live in and remedy that which they have caused. Which generation has not wished that the kings, emperors, and politicians who declare the wars, would have to come and fight in the trenches? A sense of justice is at work here. In Michener's novel, Creevey returns, but is helpless to change anything.

One of the reasons for Christ's coming was to accomplish what Creevey could not. He had not only the will but the power to change the direction in which the world was tending. Yet the redemptive act had to be real. Sin was to be taken seriously, as was the demand for justice. In addition, guilt needed an answer, as did suffering.

Servanthood and the cross are God's answer. Unlike Creevy, our Lord not only came back to survey the situation, but also He "emptied himself, taking the form of a servant" (Phil. 2:7). He could have taken the form of a king, or a general, or a chieftain, or a philosopher. Instead, he took the form of a servant. He lived out what He taught His disciples: "whoever would be first among you must be slave of all" (Mark 10:44).

Christ emptied Himself and became servant to those He had created. He did not hang on to His rights and privileges as God, but released them so we could find release in Him. He became like we are, so we could be joined to who He is. He came not to be served, but to serve. "For the Son of man also came not to be served but to serve, and to give his life as a ransom for many" (v. 45). Whatever you and I perceive about how God created all things, we have to admit He had the heavenly fortitude to come to earth and live it all out in suffering love, even unto death.

Justice and the Cross

"He became obedient unto the cross," said Paul. Nothing was worse to the first-century mind than the cross. The Roman man of letters, Cicero, said, "Let even the name of the cross be kept away from the bodies of the citizens of Rome, but also from their thought, sight, and hearing." It was regarded as an offense against good manners to speak of this hideous death in the presence of respectable people. The Son of God on the cross was, for them, a contradiction of the first order.

What was the Son of God doing on that cross?

The first thing that He was doing on the cross was providing an answer to man's demand for justice, a sense of justice built into us by God Himself. C. S. Lewis pointed out that ours is the first generation that has dared to put God on trial and accuse Him of wrongdoing.[3] Ancient man approached God as the guilty approaching the judge. For modern man, the roles are reversed. Modern man is the judge and God the judged. Intellectual arguments are not, it seems to me, a final answer to the accusations of modern man, although they may help. It is when we say with the psalmist, "Out of the depths I cry to thee, O Lord!" (Ps. 130:1), that we discover the meaning of the cross. Then we realize that the Christ of the cross found us long ago.

The Cross and the Poisons of Life

Furthermore, the cross is God's provision of making a way for us to handle the inner poisons that destroy us. Like Adam of old, when we sin, things change. Something new but destructive has come into being. Something much like poison has entered our spirits and minds. Guilt, hate, bitterness, envy, jealousy, resentment, are poisons that eat at us from the inside.

Christ handled all of these on the cross. Through theories and explanations, we keep trying to describe how this could happen. As helpful as these are, they will always be incomplete because spiritual problems have to be answered with spiritual responses, not just intellectual ones. The truth is, not even the wisest among us can explain the transformation of the heart made possible by the cross. What we do know is that whatever price needed to be paid, Christ paid for it. Whatever poisons need to be purged from our lives, the cross made possible their purging. Whatever image was needed to portray God's love, the cross painted it. Whatever proof was needed to footnote God's care, the cross penned it.

After more than thirty years as a pastor, my experience is that those who will not accept Christ's cross as an answer for their sin, wind up building a cross for themselves or someone else. They do this either by punishing themselves or someone else, usually someone who is least able to handle it. God alone is able to handle the intensity of the inner poisons that build up within us. We keep trying to make the cross a decoration. For God, it was a declaration about Himself and about His love for His world. Whatever man hands to God, trusting Him to have handled it through the cross, God hands back to man recycled, cleansed, and redeemed.

The Cross and Sacrifice

Sacrifice is a word we often apply to the cross and should. The word *sacrifice* troubles some people. They put it in the category of appeasement, as if God were exacting His "pound of flesh." But sacrifice is neither manipulation nor appeasement. Sacrifice is that which is set aside for the sake of a higher purpose. What our Lord sacrificed was not only His life on the cross but also His position as God. Our Lord "did not consider equality with God something to be grasped,/but made himself nothing" (Phil. 2:6-7, NIV). In return, we who would be transformed by Christ's gift on the cross must sacrifice some things. For the higher purpose of His healing us, we must set aside our defenses, our excuses, our blaming of others, our hiding, our self-pity, our guilt, our bitterness, our hurts, our angers, our pride. These we have tended like tender plants in our gardens of the self. We do, God help us, enjoy them. There is nothing like a good hatred to keep persons and nations revved up. But these are poisons and, like poisons, destroy life. Christ sacrificed (set aside certain things for a higher purpose) and calls from us sacrifice (setting aside some things for a higher purpose). Those who think setting aside these poisons is easy haven't been there. "He jests at scars, that never felt a wound," wrote Shakespeare.

Creator as Redeemer: A Full-Length Portrait Colossians 1:15-20

The third hymn on the Creator as Redeemer that I want us to consider is also from Paul the apostle. It has been called Paul's full-length portrait of Jesus Christ. Interestingly enough, it is found in a letter written to a church in the tiny village of Colosse. This should prove there are no insignificant churches!

> He is the image of the invisible God,
> the first-born of all creation;
> for in him all things were created,
> in heaven and on earth, visible and invisible,
> whether thrones or dominions or principalities or
> authorities—all things were created through him
> and for him.
> He is before all things,
> and in him all things hold together.
> He is the head of the body, the church; . . .
> He is the first-born from the dead, that in everything
> he might be pre-eminent.
> For in him all the fulness of God was please to dwell,
> and through him to reconcile to himself all things,
> whether on earth or in heaven,
> making peace by the blood of his cross.

I have arranged the text in this manner to better show the praise dimension of the hymn.

Creator and Sustainer

Paul made it clear that Christ was no mere prophet passing across the first-century landscape. He was in fact "before all things," and "in him all things hold together." Paul piled one preposition on top of another to draw the picture of our Lord's involvement in creation: "in him all things were created . . . through him and for him." It is not that the Creator sent Christ. Rather, the Creator was Christ. This is not just word juggling. Only the Creator can redeem. As I said earlier, redemption can only be life-giving and life-restoring if the One who is the source of life restores it.

The Image of the Creator

Christ is the "image of the invisible God," said Paul. He is our window to God, our understanding and image of what God is like. An ancient theologian named Origen spoke of the need for an image like this:

> Suppose there were a statue so immense that the eye of man could not take it all in at one look. Obviously the best way of conveying to man the lineaments of that statue would be to present man with a small copy of it in which all features would be represented on exact, smaller scale. And this is what God has done in Jesus. He has made himself intelligible by offering us a miniature of his own being. He shows us what he himself is like within the bounds of finiteness.[4]

The necessity for a clear image of God comes when we notice how often God is painted in the same hues and with the same image that people have of others or of themselves. Thus the weaknesses and flaws that we see in ourselves and others are projected upon God. We come to feel that the universe of inner personal needs is the same as the kingdom of God.

All changes in life begin with a new way of looking at things, a new image. Christ provides our new way of looking at God so that, at last, we are prepared to love Him. This is first base, first quarter, first movement, first dawn. If there is no "newness" in our vision of God, the tired images always conquer. If we see only from within ourselves, the errors in our vision continue unchecked. The witness of veteran believers is that the vision of God we see in Christ is ever new. There is always more of Him and to Him than can be explored in one lifetime. Yet, any glimpse with the response of faith is adequate to begin the adventure of loving God.

A deacon's son, often at church, was playing with a friend on the school's swing set. Higher and higher he got. The friend became concerned and warned him not to go any higher. Slowing down the young man said, "Well, Jesus will take care of me." "Who is Jesus?" his friend asked. A tough question for a young mind. Finally he replied, "I guess Jesus is the best picture of God that's ever been took." Poor grammar. Wonderful theology!

The People of the Creator-Redeemer

"He is the head of the body, the church." When we read the word *church* we often think of a building, a street corner, an address. Nothing is wrong with that. But that couldn't have been what Paul meant because no church buildings existed until decades after he lived. The reason for this was that Christianity was an illegal religion. Believers worshiped underground, often in hiding.

Church to Paul meant people, God's people. From the beginning when God designed us for relationship rather than solitary existence, others share in God's design for our lives. Through them we receive His power, love, and guidance even as we receive these things directly from Him. Anyone who reads through the Book of Acts comes to realize this. This is the church as fellowship, as *koinonia.*

The fellowship we call the church was the channel through whom salvation and blessing were to be taken to the world. God is the source of all healing, spiritual and physical, and the source of all blessing. But He chooses to send His message and the evidence of its reality through His people, who are often called His body. It is a superb analogy. Christ is the head, and the church is the body of Christ. As in physical bodies, the head is the key, the source, the starting and finishing place. But the body allows the head to carry out its functions. Without the body, the head is ineffective to carry out its purposes.

Further, the fellowship becomes the source through whom the individuals within the fellowship receive support and encouragement. Preston Taylor and I stood near an open grave recently. Preston has more memorial services than anyone I know. He is greatly loved, having served for many years as a pastor and now as an administrator of a funeral home. He said to me, "You can tell this is a Christian service." I inquired why. He said, "Look at the people; sense the spirit; watch the encouragement given. This week alone I have been at six open graves when only my staff and I were present. At the end of life this becomes clear; there is nothing to compare with the church when it is a loving, caring fellowship." Christians support each other not only in death but also in the realization that life has its traumas. Support is needed. The fellowship called the church is God's life-support system for His people.

In addition, the fellowship, the body of Christ, is the abode of the living Spirit of Christ. "Where two or three are gathered together, there I am in the midst of them," said our Lord. We experience Him in a singular and personal wav by ourselves. But the plural dimension is equally important. In truth, it is vitually impossible to sustain a vital Christian experience without this plural dimension. For in fellowship, in communion, in prayer, in sharing, in study with other believers, Christ moves and works His wonders.

That the Creator should choose to continue His spiritual creating within the body we call the church seems, on occasion, incredible. As the fellowship, we are flawed, often weak, sometimes cowardly, frequently undisciplined, and almost always underachievers. Then, suddenly, we find ourselves confronting the reality of Christ while we are together, and the miracle of His presence transforms the flaws and overrides the weaknesses. Once again, we are empowered. We know. We've once again had our blurred vision cleared. Once more we are in rhythm with Him who is our life. Things fit. Acceptance is easy. Outsiders are welcomed. We understand why Paul wrote: "To him be glory in the church and in Christ Jesus to all generations, for ever and ever. Amen" (Eph. 3:21).

The Creator and the Resurrection

"He is the beginning, the first-born from the dead." What a great foe is death. What dread it brings.

"Convince me," a person said to me, "that there is any life after death, and I will become a Christian."

"I have only two means by which to convince you," I said. "The first is the witness of the early Christians recorded in the New Testament, and the second is the experience I have in life with that same Lord they claimed was raised from the dead."

"But suppose they made it all up. Suppose they just saw a mirage or had a dream or saw a vision," he replied.

"Start with Sunday," I answered. "Suddenly, these believers who had been told never to break the sabbath, which began Friday evening and ended Saturday evening, began worshiping their Lord on Sunday, the first day of the week. There is no explanation for Sunday unless we admit something happened so overpowering that even the traditional sabbath was replaced with their own day of worship.

"Continue with their courage even unto death. People will spread a hoax, gossip, and slander. But they aren't likely to die for such. Can you imagine facing imprisonment, stonings, lions, and constant harrassment for the sake of a hoax?

"Oh, and another thing. People don't own up to gossip, to spreading stories. When confronted, they become quiet and fearful. If the resurrection is to be explained by gossip and hearsay, how do you explain these people parading up and down the world of their day spreading the good news that Christ was risen?"

"Do I have to believe in the resurrection to be a Christian?" he asked.

I nodded affirmatively and quoted Romans 10:9: "If you confess with your lips that Jesus is Lord, and believe in your heart that God raised him from the dead, you will be saved." He shook his head and we parted. Still the seed was planted. The Lord of life who draws us to Himself may yet bring another son into His family of believers. Perhaps someday he will experience that incredible resurrection kind of life which is the greatest gift of all.

He who was from the beginning, said Paul, was the first from the dead. He broke the back of death. He was the only One who could do it because He was from the beginning and knew the ending. In the last book of the Bible, Christ said, "Fear not, I am the first and the last, and the living one; I died, and behold I am alive for evermore, and I have the keys of Death and Hades" (Rev. 1:17-18). The great interrupter was interrupted. Death was dead. The resurrection of Christ is the keystone of the faith. Without that we are, as Paul said to another group of Christians, most miserable (1 Cor. 15:18).

Why is the resurrection so difficult to believe? If the Creator-Redeemer is life, then nothing He does is going to exclude life. Life is a central business of heaven. If we believe in the kind of God Jesus portrayed, eternal life is a part of His nature. We experience His life now, as well as that future dimension we have trusted to His care.

Creation as Reconciliation

"For in him all the fulness of God was pleased to dwell, and through him to reconcile to himself all things." God did not quit creating with the end of the sixth day. He continues to create by bringing back together that which once was apart. "For he is our peace, who has made us both one, and has broken down the dividing wall of hostility . . . that he might create in himself one new man in place of the two, so making peace, and might reconcile us both to God in one body through the cross, thereby bringing the hostility to an end" (Eph. 2:14-15). The greatest evidence of God's continuing activity of creation through Christ, is His constant creation of love in place of hate, and oneness in place of division. When His love is received and lived out, communion replaces alienation and caring replaces fault-finding. As His Spirit moved upon the face of the deep in the eternal beginnings, so His Spirit moves upon the face of our world seeking to bring order in the midst of chaos and reconciliation in the midst of hatred. Resistance to His activity is constant. But He never quits. And when a breakthrough happens, all heaven rejoices.

The dimensions reconciliation takes are many. One dimension of reconciliation is between the warring parts of our inner selves. We learn to love ourselves rightly, not because we are center but because we are His. In turn we find ourselves learning to love one another, even as He loved us. We even begin to learn to love those previously thought to be unloveable. Even nature becomes part of the reconciling process, and we begin to appreciate His world and respond in union with its life and rhythm.

Since we are made in God's image, we too share in the process of reconciliation as part of God's new creation. To the Corinthian Christians Paul wrote these words which tie together creation, reconciliation, and our part in God's eternal purpose: "Christ reconciled us to himself and gave us the ministry of reconciliation" (2 Cor. 5:18).

As God delegated the care of the garden to Adam long ago, so He delegates to us His grand design of reconciliation. We are called to share in the dream He had from the very dawn of creation. He could do it without us. But He has not chosen to do so. We complete what He has initiated. This is His pattern. He provides the soil, but we must till it. He provides the trees, but we must turn them into lumber, paper, or energy. He provides the water, but we must harness its power. So also in spiritual matters; He provides the gospel, but we are to share it. He has reconciled the world unto Himself, but we are to become ministers of that reconciliation. Even the sufferings of Christ need completion according to Paul. "I complete what is lacking in Christ's afflictions for the sake of his body, that is, the church" (Col. 1:24).

Lucy Chin addressed the Southern Baptist Convention in 1984 and was introduced as one who had been honored twice by her government as an adult social worker in Hong Kong. Her testimony is a beautiful witness to God's process of reconciliation as part of His continuing creation in our behalf.

Lucy was born blind. This she did not know until she was five. She was frustrated because she could not win a game she was playing. "Of course, you cannot win," said her mother, "you are blind." Later she heard neighbors discuss her plight with pity. She would have to become a prostitute when she was old enough because that was the only way blind girls could survive. There was no hope for her because she was different, sightless, a burden to her family.

The whole scene began to change when some Christians came into their home. They explained to Lucy that they knew One who cared about her, who loved everyone—Jesus Christ. In addition, they volunteered to come and take her to school where she could learn to read Braille. Thus she began the long, tedious route to getting an education. She became a Christian and began to develop an intimate relationship with the Christ who loved her. When she became a young adult, she prepared herself so that she could work with others who felt despair and hopelessness, especially the blind.

Lucy's story is the story of creation and redemption written across one life. It is the story of the Creator/Redeemer, who used His sons and daughters to effect a ministry of reconciliation in behalf of persons like Lucy. Now Lucy herself is involved in that same touch of reconciliation. Her story is different only in that her handicap is blindness. Her response to us might be, "My handicap is blindness, what's yours?" For we all have a handicap of some sort or other which needs the touch of the Savior. More often than not, He uses that handicap, now redeemed, to touch the lives of others. Once again the ministry of reconciliation lives.

Why Then?

In this chapter, we have seen the importance of understanding that God the Creator is God the Redeemer. We have sketched the dimensions of this redemption in Christ. Three hymns to Christ who was and is both Creator and Redeemer have been portrayed. We have looked at the critical need to unite in our minds God the Creator with God the Redeemer.

At this point a thoughtful person might raise some questions. Why, if God has redeemed the world, is so much trouble still left in this world? Why do bad things happen to good people? Why do innocent people suffer? Do miracles still happen? To these why-then questions, we now turn.

Notes

1. Robert Frost, "A Question," *Complete Poems of Robert Frost* (New York: Holt, Rinehart, and Winston, 1964), p. 493. Used by permission.

2. James A. Michener, *Centennial* (New York: Random House, 1974), pp. 731-830.

3. C. S. Lewis, *God in the Dock* (William B. Eerdmans Publishing Company, 1972), p. 244.

4. Quoted by John David Maguire, *The Dance of the Pilgrim* (New York: Association Press, 1967), p. 95.

10

Pain and Suffering

God created all things and then declared that it was good. Then why is there so much wrong with our world? Christ came that He might "window" for us a loving Heavenly Father and through His life, death, and resurrection, restore our relationship with Him. Then why is there still so much hatred and violence two thousand years later? How could a loving God create such a painful world? For our era, no problem stands as such a formidable barrier to Christian belief as the problem of evil and suffering. Rabbi Harold S. Kushner has dealt with his own pain and questions in *When Bad Things Happen to Good People.* It has become a bestseller. Warren W. Wiersbe's *Why Us? When Bad Things Happen to God's People* approaches the problem from an evangelical perspective. It has had wide circulation. Philip Yancey has asked, "Where is God when it hurts?" and wrote a book bearing that title. Pain is real to people.

Robert Penn Warren wrote of pain,"Oh, it is real. It is the only thing."[1] Nothing is more personal than pain. Nothing stretches the mind or demands more of faith than making sense out of suffering. We saw earlier that many have chosen to believe the whole universe to be governed by chance to explain what seems to be the irrational dimensions of pain. We also noticed that chance was no answer. It just passed the buck.

One of the dulling effects of pain and suffering is its sameness. Each year the headlines continue with painful monotony. Ancient hatreds plus modern rivalries, families in turmoil, terrorism on the increase, children starving—it all totals up to a world of pain and suffering. Yet, as sensitive or desensitized as we might become to these international caldrons of conflict, the question really hits when it hits us. As Wiersbe's title suggests, Why Me? Much cynicism that pervades our era is a response to pain, suffering, and evil.

Pain and suffering are a constant challenge to any faith which believes in a personal God who created all things. Soft, marshmallow thinking won't do. The challenge always takes two dimensions. On the one hand, the Christian must deal with the crass misunderstandings that accompany God and pain in the common mind. On the other hand, the Christian must deal with pain on a personal and experiential level. Christians hurt too.C. S. Lewis wrote one of the classics on the subject of pain. His treatise was precise, reasoned, and persuasive. It was entitled *The Problem of Pain.* But when his wife died, Lewis knew pain in new dimensions, face to face. Lewis wrote another book on pain after his wife's death. That book bore the title*A Grief Observed.* The believer's answer to suffering must be tended on two levels. The issue must be sorted out in the mind. It must also be faced within life. I hope that this chapter can touch both levels.

A good place to begin is to help the mind sort out what we are really talking about. Pain and suffering are not simple issues. The kind of natural religious responses made are too simple and inadequate to withstand the slightest tremor. We need to make a crucial distinction between natural religion and the Christian faith. Many nominal Christians have a natural view of pain, not a biblical one. Since it is natural and automatic, it is assumed to be correct. Natural religion, like a natural golf swing, oversimplifies everything and is, therefore, not much help.

Pain and Natural Religion

Every generation has within it adherents who believe in God in a natural kind of way. For them it seems comfortable to believe. It is not so much a relational commitment to God as it is a cultural affirmation. If they were interviewed in a Gallup poll, such people would say they believe in God. What natural religion does not have is a specific image of what God is like or what He is about. It has no appreciation for the risks God took at creation in granting us freedom. Nor does it have any sense of the priorities of God within creation.

Such religion is not a "revealed" religion. The biblical faith calls itself a religion of revelation because we believe that God had to correct some natural ways we look at things. In short, God must reveal what He is about; what kind of God He is; why things are like they are; and what man needs to do to change. There is no evidence that people naturally tend to believe in the God revealed in Jesus Christ.

Let us take a look at some characteristic responses natural religion makes to pain.

God as Controller

In natural religion, God is a controller. The understanding of God revealed to us in Genesis 1—3 is either ignored or considered trivial, if it is known at all. The reality of relationships and of evil and of freedom are all ignored. The almost instinctive line of reasoning goes something like this. Somewhere there must be a God. If there is a God, He must control everything that is or He wouldn't be God. Since God controls everything, when pain comes, He caused it.

Pain eventually enters all of our lives, including those from the ranks of natural religion. When pain comes, God automatically gets the blame because people assume God controls everything, including whether pain happens. For natural religion, suffering boils down to the simple issue of control.

Suppose such a person into whose life pain has entered owns his own business. He could not operate that business on the simple issue of control. If he did things would deteriorate rapidly. If no one knew the priorities of the company, work would seem worthless. If all the boss tried to do was control everything, relationships among employees would deteriorate. Without the freedom to do creative work, morale would sag. Without an understanding that everyone is not honest (that is, that evil exists), no audits would be taken, inventory checked, or time cards punched. Now, if no business could operate effectively with the single issue of control, could God's universe operate that way? The truth is, there is no reality pointed out in Genesis 2 and 3 that business does not deal with daily. Realtionships must be dealt with as must freedom, delegation, priorities, and evil. In addition, it should be pointed out that families cannot long exist when the only issue is control.

A traumatic memory from a hospital emergency room comes to me. Some teenagers had been driving while intoxicated. They hit another car. One of the teenagers was killed and one passenger from the other car also died. In the anguish of that awful aftermath a friend of the teenager who was killed saw me and exploded in anguish. "How could your God do such a thing?" It was, of course, an emotional explosion.

It was neither the time nor the place to launch into the truth of what had happened. I simply and softly stated, "My God doesn't cause accidents." But, look at it now, teenagers, who were rebelling because they thought their parents exercised too much control, had been given a measure of freedom. They had abused it and, in so doing, had caused much pain and suffereing, even death. Those teenagers would have been hostile toward any idea that God or parents had the right to restrict their freedom. But now that tragedy had ensued, God was suddenly being held accountable for not controlling everything.

Obviously, with natural religion, God is in a no-win situation. If He controls, He loses. If He doesn't control, He is to blame. The great champion of natural religion is Satan. As long as people hold to natural religion, God always gets the blame. Remember, Adam, Eve, and God were not the only realities in the garden. In addition there were these:

1. The freedom God allowed Adam and Eve;
2. The influence Adam and Eve had on each other;
3. The influence Satan had on both of them;
4. The priority of God for sons and daughters who love Him by *choice* not control; and
5. The delegation of responsibility by God to Adam.

Natural religion reduces the realities in painful situations.

Does Pain Disprove the Existence of God?

The natural response to pain can take another tack. When pain occurs the response can be: "There is no God. I suspected it all along." Prior to the pain, the person may have had doubts as to the existence of God. After the pain, the person seems to have no doubt. The equation goes something like this: Since pain is, God isn't. This kind of response is particularly evident in popular psychological materials. This underlying equation is the same: A loving God could not exist because the world is painful. This is, of course, a poor rationale for unbelief. It is like saying that loving parents do not exist because we can observe that all children suffer, experience pain, and sometimes do evil things. Obviously this is a simplistic solution. One could just as easily argue that since all children suffer pain, all parents are child abusers. Obviously, some factors have been omitted in this kind of reasoning. The view that natural man has of God, life, and pain is too simple for the complexity of any painful situation.

With such a simplistic approach to pain, natural religion winds up with the conclusion that either God does not exist or that He is absent from His world. In the biblical account, pain, which was caused by Adam's choice not by God's, does not cause God's exit. Neither the errant choice nor the pain drove God from the garden or out of His world. Nor does it close the book on His presence within His creation. In fact, God sought Adam and Eve, establishing at least a question and answer relationship with them: "Where are you, Adam?" Adam's choice, which caused the painful experience of shame, became the catalyst whereby God confronted Adam. In this instance, God's power did not take the dimension of control, but of loving confrontation.

Some Important Distinctions

One way to move away from the too-simple approach of natural religion is to begin to make some distinctions.

Types of Pain

First, there is *natural* pain. This involves some disease, natural destructive events, such as tornados, some birth defects, and the like. Second, there is *willful* pain. Adam's pain was caused because of Adam's choice. Third, there is *relational* pain. Adam and Eve influenced each other. They were vulnerable to one another. Pain which is caused by relational trauma can be the most painful of all. Divorce, desertion, neglect, and outright abuse are only a few of the ways in which we humans inflict pain on one another. We rightly call our memories of these "painful," full of pain.

Fourth, there is pain caused by *evil.* The serpent in the garden was delighted to cause the pain but shrewd enough to try to escape the blame. Fifth, there is pain caused by *freedom.* Freedom is an awesome planet revolving around life. Two of its stellites are chance and accident. It is impossible, humanly speaking, to think of freedom without eventually thinking of chance and accident. And it is impossible to think of chance and accident without thinking of freedom. In some theologies, chance and accident are removed by making God responsible for everything. To do this, however, both evil and freedom have to be removed from the human situation. The Genesis insights have to be shelved.

Determinism and Freedom

Predestination and human freedom have been debated through the centuries. They are similar to a parallel that exists in natural science. Both the wave theory and the particle theory of the nature of light can be proved. On the one side is convincing evidence that light is indeed a wave phenomenon and that electrons are particles. At the same time, equally convincing evidence exists that light consists of discrete particles and that electrons are true waves. Applications can be made which support both sides of the theory. Yet, they can't be proved at the same time. Both can be proved to be true. Yet one would seem to exclude the other. They are a true natural paradox. Freedom and predestination are paradoxical. Theologically both can be shown to be true. Yet, neither can be proved at the same time. Thomas Aquinas wrote: "Nothing which implies contradiction falls under the omnipotence of God."[2]

Practically speaking, however, we live with both. There is a determined side of our lives. There is also an undetermined side. We live not only with a sense of chosenness but with the reality of accident and chance. Dorothy Sayers once remarked that "even the most thoroughgoing philosophic determinist will swear at the maid . . . when the toast is burned."[3]

The trouble develops for faith when only one half of the paradox is truly believed, for instance, only that of predestination. Then God is held responsible for everything that happens from Hitler's death camps to cancer. Several years ago two researchers from the University of Chicago and Southern Illinois University studied victims of tornado damage across the country. They found people in the South suffered a higher frequency of tornado-related deaths than Midwesterners, even after taking into account such factors as differences in building materials. After scrutinizing Alabamians and Illinoisans, the researchers concluded that Southerners, being more religious, had developed a fatalistic attitude toward disaster:"If it hits, it hits, and there's nothing I can do to stop it." In contrast Midwesterners listened to weather reports and sought out safe places.[4] Amazing. What those researchers bumped into was a group of people who lived by only one-half of the paradox of the human situation. As always, what we believe about creation ripples down to the most practical side of life.

Does this mean that God can't do anything about pain? No, of course not. What it means is that freedom is real and not an illusion. So is evil. So is the pain caused by relationships. All of these are so real, in fact, that they meant for God a cross and a crown of thorns.

Pain and Miracles

When we think about pain, we often bump into the subject of miracles. If God has the power to do miracles, why doesn't He do something about the suffering in the world? Of course, such a question comes at us from a certain corner. That corner assumes that pain is evil and must necessarily be done away with. It further assumes that God's power could best be used for this purpose. Before tackling those questions, we should take a look at the importance of miracles in the first place. Not all agree that miracles can happen.

The Importance of Miracles for the Christian

The Christian faith was birthed from a miracle we call the resurrection of Jesus Christ. In the Book of Acts, which includes the earliest recorded sermons of the church, the resurrection was the central theme of every one of them. Later the significance of the cross was seen and experienced. Eventually the early believers began to see that the Creator and Redeemer were one and the same. The Gospels and the Letters were written, which we find in the New Testament. But in the beginning was the resurrection of Jesus. This was the gospel, the good news, and everything else protruded like spokes from this center.

Some liberal theology speaks of the resurrection as a later addition. Such thinking starts by taking a few of the nice sayings from the Gospels. Then it is thought that the rest of Christian belief evolved in an effort to explain things and make them look supernatural. Historically, this is not the sequence in which it happened. The resurrection was first. Indeed this was the first qualification for apostleship. Paul said, "Am I not an apostle? Have I not seen Jesus our Lord?" (1 Cor. 9:1). Paul began his defense of the resurrection with a listing of those who witnessed the resurrection (1Cor. 15). If these had died without persuading others to believe this gospel of the resurrection of Jesus, the rest of the New Testament would never have come into being. This ultimate new beginning of the resurrection, this grandest of our inaugural events, is a miracle or it is nothing. This is the pivot around which all Christian faith revolves. If this is true, everything else falls into place. If not, it all falls. "If Christ has not been raised, your faith is futile and you are still in your sins. But in fact Christ has been raised from the dead" (1 Cor. 15:17,20).

For the Christian faith then, miracles are not an addendum. This is not to say the Christian has to believe every advertisement today that a miracle has taken place. Perhaps nothing is more open to manipulation and misinterpretation than miracles. But at the core of the faith are the great central events, all of which are miracles: creation, the incarnation, the atonement, the resurrection, and the second coming of Christ.

The Rejection of the Miraculous

For some people, miracles are impossible because nature is thought to run on precise and inflexible laws. To use C. S. Lewis's phrase, nature is the Whole Show.[5] It is the All. It is the Everything. It is the whole truth about whatever is. Futhermore, such a view would see the many laws of nature so intertwined and interlocked that each depends upon the other. Miracles would suggest an interruption of these observable laws and, therefore, an impossibility. Concerning this viewpoint three things need to be said.

First, nature is not that simple. Classical physics did tend to portray the natural world in terms of utter predictability. This is no final argument against miracles even if it were true. As we saw in the earlier chapter on "Beginnings," miracles happen within the predictable. But physics has enlarged its viewpoint since those early days when everything was thought to run on an utterly predictable track. Quantum mechanics, which is a part of physics, has given scientists a new set of glasses through which to look. To oversimplify for the sake of brevity, classical physics said, "This is the way things are." Quantum mechanics would answer, "It's not quite that simple." In an article entitled "The Quantum Theory and Reality," Bernard d'Espagnat states, "The doctrine that the world is made up of objects whose existence is independent of human consciousness turns out to be in conflict with quantum mechanics and with facts established by experiment."[6]

An illustration from quantum mechanics might help. A radioactive form of the element iodine is widely used now in the treatment of certain physical disorders. Every radioiodine atom has open to it two alternatives. It may either remain in its present state and continue as a radioiodine atom, or it may explosively change one of its neutrons into a proton by emitting appropriate radiation and become a xenon atom. The quantum mechanical theory is that all that can be specified about the behavior of a radioiodine atom is the probability that it will make this choice in a given period of time. No forces, external or internal, known or unknown, can eliminate the element of choice or chance from the picture. Physicians know how much of a dose of radioiodine should be administered because probabilities can be computed with some precision. After all in one dose may be a hundred million billion radioiodine atoms. But quantum mechanics would insist that in dealing with one atom of radioiodine the most that can be predicted with certainty is how long it will take for the alternative to be chosen. The point is that alternatives exist within the nature of even the smallest particles of nature.[7]

Second, we don't fit comfortably within nature.—If nature is the Whole Show, then we should fit comfortably in our niches within it. In fact, we don't. We are continually rearranging it. If we live where it is cold, we invent ways to warm things up. We build navigational systems, split atoms, fill teeth, operate on diseased bodies, and build space vehicles. Unlike animals that seem to find their niches and fit within nature, we keep trying to rearrange things for the better. It is as if some inner voice from some primeval past keeps whispering, "Subdue it" (Gen. 1:28).

Third, we transcend nature.—If nature and its laws are the All, we should feel ourselves immersed in it. In fact, we don't. We have a transcendent dimension to us. For example, you can, at this minute put this book aside and imagine yourself in miniature sitting on a shelf looking at yourself and everything in the room. You can, in short, rise above the surroundings you are in and perceive the whole scene as a spectator.

When it comes to nature, we are often not so much a part of it as we are spectators watching it. Sometimes we feel completely apart from it. If other parts of creation have this capability, we have no evidence of it. Fish seem content to be fish; bears are content to hibernate in winter; and birds migrate to warmer climates in winter. They are comfortable within nature. They are part of it and its rhythms. We are watchers. We are confused even about our own rhythms. We are transcendent beings.

These three reasons do not prove miracles happen, of course. They simply open things up. They suggest that the natural world is not as fixed in place as once thought, nor are we within it.

Miracle and Method

As methodical people, we feel most comfortable when we understand methods. Tinkering with the "hows" of the universe is one of the things we do best. The trouble with miracles is that we don't know miracles by their method but by their result. Luci Shaw caught this truth in her poem.

> No, He is too quick. We never
> Catch Him at it. He is there
> sooner than our thought, our prayer.
> Searching
> backward, we cannot discover *how*
> or get inside the miracle.
>
> Even if it were here and now
> how would we describe the just-born trees
> swimming into place at their green creation,
> flowering upward in the air
> with all their thin twigs quivering
> in gusts of grace? or the great
> white whales fluking
> through crystalline seas
> like recently inflated balloons? Who could
> time the beat of a man's heart
> as the woman comes close enough to fill
> his newly-hollow side? Who will
> diagram the gynecology
> of incarnation, the trigonometry of trinity?
> or chemically analyse wine
> from a well? or see inside
> joints as they loosen, and whole limbs
> and lives? Will anyone stand beside
> the moving stone? and plot the bright
> trajectory of the ascension? and explain
> the tongues of fire
> telling both heat and light?
>
> Enough. Refrain.
> Observe a finished work. Think:
> Today—another miracle—the feathered

arrow of my faith may link
God's bow and target.[8]

The closest we can come is to understand the paradox of miracles. They happen within, yet are new. The virgin birth did not intrude upon the natural processes of birth. Nothing was displaced or discarded, not even interrupted. The paradox is that within the predictable processes of the physical world, within some alternative known only to God, the invisible Power touched the visible reality. Miracle happened. Jesus was conceived by the power of the Holy Spirit and was born to a virgin named Mary. Thus we see the paradox of how the invisible Power touched the visible reality.

Christ and Miracles

Miracles permeated the ministry of Jesus. Rarely, however, are His miracles described as "wonders." Instead, they are commonly described as "powers" or "signs."[9] The miracles of Jesus are not those of a magician. They are evidences of the kind of person He is. They are "signs" of His care, of His faithfulness, of His compassion. Thus the guiding principle in Jesus' miracles is not in the rearranging of matter, but in the portrayal of His person.

Christ's miracles do not draw us to Him. His person, who He is draws us. Miracles have their rightful place, as do tulips in the spring. But like the tulips are bright evidences of spring, miracles are bright evidences of a greater wonder, Christ Himself.

Miracles and Pain

Miracles, then, are not avenues of escape from the trials of life nor the pain experienced on the journey. They are signposts pointing to the caring of the personal Lord. Caring may, however, take many forms. The easing of pain is just one of them. Sometimes intervention is not the answer.

Miracles and Trust

Even as miracles can mirror the faithfulness of God, so can the absence of miracles mirror His faithfulness. At stake here is trust. trust cannot exist without solid predictability. A wife who cannot trust her husband cannot do so because his behavior is unpredictable. A parent who cannot trust a teenager cannot do so because a commitment does not cement a predictable response. If God is to be trusted, He must also be predictable. He is not going to rearrange the universe simply to ease our pain. He is not going to trespass our freedom of choice even though the choices sometimes bring painful harvests. His refusal to interrupt, which means His decision not to intervene, may be one of the greatest evidences of His care. Only the God who stays with His predictables can be trusted.

Our inner demand for God to intervene in a world of pain is emotional rather than rational. Suppose God interrupted all of the policies and laws by which creation runs simply to allievate some distress, trivial or unthinkable. Such a world would be loveless, freedomless, and formless. Most of all, it would never accomplish what God has in mind for us.

God's Priority for Us

One assumption of secular society is that we humans are mostly finished, fully matured creatures. Like graduates of a finishing school who have been prepared for all of the nice things of life, we deserve a nice world to live in. Pain is, therefore, one of the first nuisances, or evils, to be gotten rid of.

Such a picture certainly doesn't come from the Scripture. The apostle Peter wrote to the early Christians:

> Beloved, do not be surprised at the fiery ordeal which comes upon you to prove you, as though something strange were happening to you. But rejoice in so far as you share Christ's sufferings, that you may also rejoice and be glad when his glory is revealed. (1 Pet. 4:12-13).

Nothing was finished for the apostle. Suffering was not to be taken as something strange that was happening to them. In the Bible, we don't get the picture of a beautifully finished mosaic. We get the picture of a world full of scrambles and scribbles. We get the picture of a mankind with a crazy-quilt mixture of saintliness and scoundrel, of cruelty and tenderness, a mankind that desperately needs some basic reworking.

Unfortunately, what mankind seems best at doing is tinkering with the physical world. He seems much less inclined to face up to the fact that the development of his inner person has lagged far behind his technology. Instead of being a product of a finishing school ready for the nice things of life, he seems spiritually and relationally retarded.

M. Scott Peck says it is a human characteristic to avoid the pain of challenge.[11]

If our inner spiritual and relational selves are laggard, we ought to find the Creator giving us a universe to jar us out of that "inner laziness." That is, in fact, what we find. Since even the smallest particles of the atom are the concern of the Creator, we may assume the smallest item of life can be used by Him to help us grow. His priority is not so much to make us painless as to help our development as persons. He wills our fullness and our growth, because He loves us. Maturity reflects both. A universe that demands nothing from us is not likely to produce that desired result.

The chaplain was telling me about how painful it was to watch. A young man who had been pitched from a horse had been paralyzed. Slowly, but surely he had begun to respond. He had gone to the huge regional hospital for further therapy. On the day he was to take his first step, the people who helped him stand stood aside. He fell flat on his face. He wept in pain. Nobody moved. The chaplain, friend and confidant of the family, felt every instinctive push to rush to his aid. But the therapists would not let him. Again the boy tried. Again the agony of the fall and the defeat. Again and again the cruelty continued, for it could indeed have been called that. Pain was the product of the whole occasion. Every part of the experience was painful. It was dreadfully painful to the young man. It was painful to the therapists who watched. It was painful to the chaplain who empathized.

But the boy walked! The day came when he walked! It all depends, you see, on one's priority. By contrast, there was a cartoon I remember with a mother helping her son into a wheelchair. A nearby friend said, "I didn't know your son coundn't walk." The reply: "Oh, he can. But thank God he doesn't have to." From everything we know in the Scripture, God is not like that mother. He is more like the therapists. He wants us to walk and run and soar. He is about the business of soulmaking. If He needs to work through this stained, bent-out-of-shape world we live in, He will. His will for us is not to make us happy or unhappy. It is to make us, us, as only He knows we can be. To will for us fullness and growth, He weaves into the tapestry of our lives both joy and pain. He will not give up "until we all attain to the unity of the faith and of the knowledge of the Son of God, to mature manhood, to the measure of the stature of the fullness of Christ" (Eph. 4:13).

The Positive Side of Pain

Pain is, for our age, almost synonomous with evil. Paradoxically, God, more than the devil, gets blamed for it. The mountains of drugs consumed each year bear witness to the fact that our age has little patience with pain of any kind. Alcoholism is often a result of the pain of emptiness, as is drug abuse.

To say that pain is always wrong is much too simple. For example, pain has a protective dimension which is positive and essential. A good place to begin appreciating the positive side of pain is by looking at our physical bodies.

Pain in the Body

In his book *Where Is God When It Hurts?* Philip Yancey has done us a favor by doing some research into the whole matter of physical pain.[12] Much of it comes from his friend Dr. Paul Brand. Yancey describes Brand as the only man he knows of who crusades in behalf of pain. Brand's announcement is, "Thank God for inventing pain! I don't think he could have done a better job. It's beautiful."[13] Dr. Brand works with lepers. Leprosy attacks the nervous system. Lepers feel no pain. They no longer have that gift.

Brand's appreciation for pain climaxed after he was given a grant to design an artificial pain system for the human body. He hoped to help people for whom disease had destroyed the pain sensors in their bodies.

To begin with, Brand had to think like the Creator. He had to anticipate the needs of the body. After signing on some research professionals—one in electronic engineering, one who was a bioengineer, and several research biochemists—he began. First, a glove was invented which responded to pressure with an electric current which stimulated a warning signal. For five years Dr. Brand and his assistants tackled the technical problems. The more they studied, the more complex their task appeared. At what level would the sensor sound a warning? How could a sensor distinguish between the normal pressure of gripping a railing and the pressure of gripping a thornbush? How could they allow for touch activities, such as tennis playing, and yet warn of danger.

Brand also noticed that nerve cells change to meet the situation the body is in. Sometimes the pain signals are really turned up to a high volume. Bumps and bruises become ten times as sensitive as normal. That's why a swollen finger feels awkward and in the way.

The more they worked the more impossible their job seemed to be. All the artificial sensors proved fragile and would rupture or fail from metal fatigue or corrosion after a few hundred uses. Brand and his associates gained more and more appreciation for the remarkable engineering of the body's pain network.

After five years of work, thousands of man-hours, and a million dollars, Dr. Brand and his associates abandoned the entire project. A warning system suitable for just one hand was exorbitantly expensive, subject to frequent mechanical breakdowns, and hopelessly inadequate to interpret the mass of sensations the hand encounters. The system sometimes called "God's great mistake" was far too complex for even the most sophisticated technology to imitate. God's design of the pain network is not an accident. It is not God's great goof, and it is not an afterthought. It fits us well.

Pain from Life

Paul lived with pain most of his life. He asked for relief. "Three times I besought the Lord about this, that it should leave me; but he said to me, 'My grace is sufficient for you, for my power is made perfect in weakness' " (2 Cor. 12:8-9). Paul's pain, God told him, had a positive purpose. Life is God's great workshop. Since pain is part of life, even as joy is, God uses pain on occasion to work in all things for our growth and our good.

Sometimes pain gets our attention.—C. S. Lewis wrote, "God whispers to us in our pleasures, speaks in our conscience, but shouts in our pains: it is His megaphone to rouse a deaf world."[14] Pain always causes some kind of response. Pain is an interrupter. It does get attention. Sometimes the response is negative. Bitterness develops. Other times the Word is heard and a new acceptance of one's need and God's grace occurs.

"I've got to talk to somebody." she said. "I pass by the church here on my way to work. I thought maybe you could see me and that's why I called. I've got to talk to someone. I can't go on like I am. I used to go to church all the time when I was young. Then . . ." Change a few words and this is an introduction that pastors hear again and again. The pattern is familiar. The secular cocoon has claimed a convert. Pain is often the prompter, the megaphone God uses to break through the destructive cocoon in which we have wrapped ourselves.

Sometimes God uses pain to remind us of our common human bonding.—One thing that has always struck me as unique about an intensive care waiting room is that all the people there are on the same level. Some are rich, some are poor. Some are local people, some are not. Some are white, some are black. Some are young, some are old. All are in the same fix. They are there because pain, in one form or another, has entered their lives. Pain is a great leveler. I have seen executives weep because of the heartbreak of a custodian. In an intensive care ward, you realize there really is a family of mankind. Pain can't bring love and compassion, but it can create an openness for it.

Karl Olsson has written about God's renewal on the ground level of human need in *Meet Me on the Patio.*[15] He says that we get caught in the trap of rising through life like floors ascending up a tower. We talk to others on that same level. We think renewal is there. It isn't. It's on ground level. On ground level all humanity meets with a tear in the eye, dealing with the same raw, basic personal hurts. At the foot of the cross, everyone is equal. Sometimes it takes pain to remind us of that.

Sometimes pain deepens.—The theologian was of national, even international fame. He was in town for reasons of a lectureship. A group of ministers were invited to attend. Interestingly enough, we talked little theology. We talked a lot about life. This man of theological fame had lived in almost constant pain for years. Recent surgery had helped some. But the pain would never go completely away. As he talked, it was obvious that the experience had done something personally and spiritually that theological understanding could never have done. He spoke in quiet terms of being sustained through it all by the presence of God. A kind of inner surgery had taken place. Nonessentials had been cut away. An inner confidence born of faith refined through trial had occurred. He said, "I sometimes think I could stand almost anything anymore. Which is to say, I live more free of fear and anxiety than I ever have. I have learned the meaning of trust in and patience with a God who has let me hurt continually, yet has loved me completely." Those of us who were invited had come to deal with rational issues of theology. Instead we found ourselves confronted by the experience of a man whose depth and compassion had been born out of adversity. His words carried importance because his life was authentic and real. It was as if all the dross had been burned out.

Sometimes pain signals something positive is happening.—Inner pain results any time the self-centered ego has to make room for something other than "please me." Love which wills the best for another at the expense of selfish comfort may cause pain. Any time space is made in the self for God instead of the please-me selfish ego, pain resluts. Any person who can be described as accepting (full of grace), instead of judgmental (full of condemnation), has experienced some inner, spiritual surgery. Some things have been cut out, and others inserted. We have often called this dimension, "growing pains." We learn from experience, even though those lessons are often painful. Paul said to the Roman Christians? "We rejoice in our sufferings, because we know that suffering produces perserverance; perserverance, character; and character, hope. And hope does not disappoint us, because God has poured out his love into our hearts by the Holy Spirit, whom he has given us," (Rom. 5:3-5, NIV).

A Word of Caution

Read carefully a word of caution, please. Pain is not the object of the Christian faith, joy is. Having made a case for the way God uses pain, we could easily misunderstand what faith is all about. Pain, for pain's sake, is sickness. But the basic choice for Adam and for all of us since is whether God will be the center of our lives or whether we will. Dislodging the stubborn, clinging, defensive, judgmental, evasive, God-playing self from the center of life is painful. Making a place for God, joy, love, and peace to reside means something has to go. Spiritual surgery, like physical surgery, is painful.

Other Questions About Pain

Is God the Author of Pain?

Make a distinction between original cause and secondary cause. Are parents responsible for all of the pain their children experience? They are the procreators of those children, the original cause. But their children have wills of their own. Space must be put between original cause and secondary cause on both the human and divine level. Otherwise the integrity of the will is forfeited. Since God is the

Creator of all things, He is the original cause. But when He willed for us wills, He took the risks of secondary causes of pain. Much pain is caused by secondary willful and relational behavior.

Why Doesn't God Punish Willful Wrong Immediately?

Why does God wait until the final judgment? Think what a deterrant to evil it would be if every time we erred we would be instantly punished. The body does this, why not the soul? It certainly would tidy things up.

For God this would be counterproductive. We would behave. But we would behave for self-centered reasons of escaping pain. Would parents rather have children love them because they have chosen to or because they are afraid not to? The priority of the Father in heaven is for sons and daughters who have looked all of the options full in the face and still have chosen to love Him.

Is Pain Punishment for Sin?

Just as the body has built into it some pain sensors, so also does the soul. Remorse, guilt, and shame are some inner pain sensors. They protect. They warn. They also reflect the moral law built into us. Like physical laws that are violated, transgression of moral law brings pain. In this sense, sin punishes.

Jesus said to the woman caught in adultery, "Neither do I condemn thee, go, and sin no more" (John 8:11, KJV). Mercy and not punishment permeate heaven. David said, "He knows our frame; he remembers that we are dust" (Ps. 103:14). Job's accusers wrongly tried to link Job's suffering with punishment for sin. When Jesus was confronted with this same question, He refused to equate punishment with sin (Luke 13:1-5). The central issue was not punishment, He said, but repentance.

Every system has to have some policies, to operate God's world is no exception. At the office, violation of the policies does not reflect the character of the boss but the character of the offender. We need to be sure we make a distinction between the policies of creation, the character of the offender, and the character of the Creator.

Does the Devil Cause Pain?

Absolutely. Go back to Adam, Eve, and the serpent. Or examine Jesus' argument with the Pharisees about healing on the sabbath. He said, " And ought not this woman, a daughter of Abraham whom Satan bound for eighteen years, be loosed from this bond on the sabbath day?" (Luke 13:16). Or go to twentieth-century Germany. The same country which produced Bach, Beethoven, Luther, Goethe, and Brahms also gave us Hitler, Eichmann, and Goering.

Why Does God Permit Natural Evil?

Natural evil, remember, incluses some disease, tornadoes, some birth defects, and so forth. How could a loving God permit such to happen? What we forget is that nature has yet to be redeemed. The world, Paul said is in travail. It is awaiting redemption. It is yearning for release and rebirth. (Rom. 8:18-25).

For centuries theologians have spoken of creation and man as fallen. The will God willed for Adam, and for us, has been abused and misdirected. The creature enthroned himself as center. When the Creator was dethroned, things quickly began to deteriorate. It was like the custodians suddenly had taken over the surgical unit at the hospital. They loved their position, but havoc resulted. Death became the bottom line. This is the picture painted by Scripture after the fall. The world is a rebel. The crown jewel of freedom has been used to scratch and deface the surface of the earth. "We talk of wild animals," says Chesterton, "but man is the only wild animal. It is man that has broken out."[16] Nature reflects the awful result.

As for why God doesn't straighten everything out, we come back to His priorities. He has chosen to accept the risks of creating a world where people can love or reject Him freely. This freedom misused has caused the world to go tilt. Nothing works exactly right. A phychiatrist, M. Scott Peck, remarked: "It is a strange thing. Dozens of times I have been asked by patients or acquaintances: ' Dr. Peck, why is there evil in the world?' Yet no one has ever asked me in all these years: 'Why is there good in the world?' It is as if we automatically assume this is a naturally good world that has somehow been contaiminated by evil."[17] The original memory remains. Yet we are part of a stained world. It is a major setback. But God is not going to renounce His original purpose even if it means a world of pain and suffering.

People say, "That's not fair. Why doesn't He come down and see what it is like." That, of course, is what Christians say has happened.

The Pain of God

So He came. The One through whose breath the worlds were made had to gasp for His first breath. Birth. The trauma of birth. He who knew the dimensions of the galaxies and saw the sun as but a stone in His immense universe, needed the warmth of a manger to keep Him warm on inaugural night. He who engineered the process by which plants could grow, seeds sprout, and grain be harvested, needed a mother's breast to survive. The one who watched it all develop was taking upon Himself the whole process.

A noted television personality explaining why he became disillusioned with Christianity, asked, "How could an all-knowing God allow His Son to be murdered on a cross in order to redeem my sins? If God the Father is so all-loving', why didn't He come down and go to Calvary?"[18] The answer is, He did. Christians have never said, whatever their denomination, that Christ was the "son" of God, like our three sons are our sons by procreation. *Son* means likeness, like son and daughter look like the parents. God is one. Our Christian doctrine of the Trinity is our effort to try and explain the three distinct dimensions of God we know through our Christian experience. Through the Spirit of God, Christ the Son came within life to mirror the reality of the Father. If it seems complex, experience is complex, and words are frail vehicles to describe it. *Son* is the word chosen from the earliest to express God's entrance into human life to portray the likeness of the Father. You may look for a better title to describe what Christ was doing, but I doubt you will find it. The important thing here is to sense God's *entering in.*

What the Savior did in that incredible event we call the incarnation was to so immerse Himself in the human situation that He came to know every crease, every fold of it so He might confront us with the Father's will at every point. Like an explorer out to chart the terrain, He climbed its peaks, roamed its monotonous plateaus, and descended into its cavernous valleys. Like a spelunker entering the darkness of an unexplored cave, He lowered himself into the possiblilities that encased the human situation. Like a child on a hillside, he explored the beauty of the flowers, watched the sparrows dart here and there, and charted the blooming time of the lilies.

The seasons passed, and He took upon Himself the responsibliity of a carpenter. But one day that carpenter, that gnarled-handed, bruised-fingered carpenter, set aside his hammer to assume the mantle of human leadership. The whole gamut was His—recruiting, training, developing, delegating, planning, motivating, and administrating. The awful pressures of eternal leadership compressed not into one lifetime, but into three years—three pressure-cooker years to prepare some fisherman, a tax collector, a Zealot, and other nondescripts to carry on the kingdom He said was not of this world.

No sooner had He spoken His first sermon than people knew He wouldn't leave things alone. He would change them. Their hatred was born for the One who insisted they were rotting in their status quo. From then on, the criticism never stopped. It turned to hatred and finally to vengeance. One would have thought that the church of His day would have lent some support. But they had no time for One whose gospel trumpeted out good news instead of religious legalism. They never got off of His back. They rode it to the end.

Like the universe He created, He reveled in ordered freedom. Those who only saw in Him freedom were always disappointed and those who saw in Him only order were disillusioned. When He laughed, they frowned. When He frowned, they laughed. "Why can't He adjust?" asked His neighbors. "Why can't he go back to carpentering?" asked His townsmen. "You know He could have been the best carpenter in Nazareth. What a waste." One of the deepest hurts is to be misunderstood by family, friends, and peers. He never entirely fit anyone's mold. Which means He never enjoyed the safety of any human group while He walked into territory not even His disciples understood.

The Chinese language combines the two words *love* and *pain* in one eloquent drawing. In the character that expresses the highest kind of love, symbols for love and for pain are brushed on top of each other to create a word like "pain-love."[19] A chinese mother can be said to pain-love her child. During those days, and in all days since, in ways not even God had experienced before, the Creator pain-loved His creation. All of it. There was no hesitation to His touch, nor is there now. No hesitancy, not even with the lepers.

His voice echoed over the dimensions of His creation, calling it back to center, to health, to itself, to Him. The call wrapped itself around every nook and cranny of that bent-out-of-shape creation and felt the impulse of the Creator's pain-love. No one got lost in the crowd: the hungry, the thirsty, the down-and out, the up-and out, the lepers, the crippled, the blind, the workers, the masters, the leaders, the followers, the sick, the imprisoned—all in one way or another feeling pain. These He called to Himself to show them the Father. Even with the long list, we have but touched the surface, for we have dealt with visible pain. What of the invisible? What of the lonely, the guilty, the rejected, the angry, the vengeful, the grief-stricken, the empty? All of the pain corners of creation felt the impulse of the pain-love of the Creator being shown in His Son. After He was here we knew, knew from core and being, that there would be no manipulation, no pressure, no coercion. Pain-love was not a new gimmic. It was the Creator calling people whom He loves more even than His life to find again its source of being, its roots, its center. Only the choice had to be made freely.

Did the Creator love His creation even more than His life? Look at His cross. See the crucified Son of God.

The cup of humanity's pain, Jesus drank to the full. With gasps, He whispered words that pain-loved His world right up to the last. "Father, forgive them." "Behold your son; behold your mother." "I thirst." He conquered death, pain, and hell not with a sledge hammer, but with His own vulnerable pain-loving.

So don't, pray don't, wiggle down in your nice, little nest with central air and heat, a full stomach, a closet full of clothes and ask nice little questions about "Where was God when . . . ." G. K. Chesterton knew where God was when he wrote symbolically:

> "I see everything," he cried, "everything that there is. Why does each thing on the earth war against each other thing? Why does each small thing in the world have to fight against the world itself? Why does a fly have to fight the whole universe? . . .For the same reason that I had to be alone in the dreadful Council of Days . . . So that the real lie of Satan may be flung back in the face of this blasphemer, so that by tears and torture we may earn the right to say to this man, 'You lie!' No agonies can be too great to buy the right to say to this accuser, 'We also have suffered.' "
>
> He had turned his eyes so as to see suddenly the great face of Sunday, which wore a strange smile.
>
> 'Have you," He cried in a dreadful voice, "Have you ever suffered?"
>
> As he gazed, the great face grew to an awful size . . . he seemed to hear a distant voice saying a commonplace text that he had heard somewhere, "Can ye drink of the cup that I drink of?"[20]

Somewhere, sometime, shed a tear for a world that may never know Him or life because it is terrified of pain.

We shrink from the struggle and forfeit the joy.

But of course, eternal life doesn't die and didn't. The One who pain-loved His world until it cost Him a cross lives. No Judean tomb could keep Him any more than Nazareth could. Gustaf Aulen called Him *Christus Victor*. Christ the victor. He is the victor over pain, suffering, chance, sin, accident, rejection, slander, even the grave.

He still walks among us, pain-loving as He goes. He *knows*. He always knew. But now He *knows*. And He did this for your benefit and mine.

Knowing Him makes the eternal difference. Such *knowing* makes these the most incredible words ever written about the joys and pains of life? "We *know* that in everything God works for good with those who love him, who are called according to his purpose" (Rom. 8:28, author's italics).

His last, first, and always words to His disciples never change. "I will be with you always, to the very end of the age." (Matt. 28:20, NIV.) He never leaves, even as He never left. Even when the clouds of life on occasion blot out the sun but do not detract from its existence, so He remains constant. The gift no money can buy and only trust can *know* is the greatest gift of all, the presence of the living God, Creator of heaven and earth.

Notes

1. Quoted by Huston Smith, *The Religions of Man* (New York: Mentor Books, 1958), p. 108.
2. Quoted by C. S. Lewis, *The Problem of Pain* (London: Geoffrey Bles, 1943), p. 14.
3. William G. Pollard, *Chance and Providence* (New York: Charles Scribner's, 1958), P. 124.
4. Philip Yancey, *Where Is God When It Hurts?* (Grand Rapids: Zondervan Publishing House, 1977), p. 72.
5. C. S. Lewis, *Miracles*, (New York: Macmilan, 1963), p. 10.
6. Bernard d'Espagnat, "The Quantum Theory and Reality," *Scientific American*, Vol. 241, No. 5, Nov. 1979, pp. 158.
7. Pollard, pp. 51-52.

8. Quoted by James M. Houston, *I Believe in the Creator* (Grand Rapids: William B. Eerdmans Publishing Company, 1980), pp. 45-6.

9. *Ibid.,* p. 102.

10. Yancey, p. 75.

11. M. Scott Peck, *The Road Less Traveled* (New York: Simon and Schuster, 1978), p. 56.

12. Yancey, pp. 23-29.

13. *Ibid.,* p. 23.

14. C. S. Lewis, *The Problem of Pain* (London: Geoffrey Bles, 1943), p. 81.

15. Karl Olsson, *Meet Me on the Patio* (Minneapolis: Augsburg, 1977).

16. G. K. Chesterton, *Orthodoxy* (Garden City, New Jersey: Doubleday and Company, Inc. 1959), p. 144.

17. Scott Peck, *People of the Lie,* (New York: Simon and Schuster, 1983), p. 41.

18. Quoted in Dr. Paul Brand and Philip Yancey, *In His Image* (Grand Rapids, Michigan: Zondervan Publishing House, 1984), p. 285

19. *Ibid.,* p. 282.

20. G. K. Chesterton, *The Man Who Was Thursday* (Bristol: J. W. Arrowsmith, 1944), pp. 190-191.

Index